AEROBIC DANCING

ÆROBIC

Dancing

By **JACKI SORENSEN**

With **BILL BRUNS**

Photographs by

JASMINE LINDSAY

RAWSON, WADE PUBLISHERS, INC.
New York

Even if you feel you're ready to dance on Broadway, it makes good sense—and it's absolutely necessary—that you check with your doctor before undertaking *any* exercise program.

Library of Congress Cataloging in Publication Data

Sorensen, Jacki.
  Aerobic dancing.

  Includes indexes.
  1. Aerobic exercises.   2. Dancing.
I. Bruns, Bill, joint author.   II. Title.
RA781.15.S67   613.7'1   79-64207
ISBN 0-89256-110-6
ISBN 0-89256-115-7 pbk.

Published simultaneously in Canada by McClelland and Stewart, Ltd.
Manufactured in the United States of America

Designed by Jacques Chazaud

First Edition

CONTENTS

For Mommy
and all other Aerobic Dancers.

With special thanks to
my loving husband, Neil, and
my friend Pat, who do so much
to make my dreams come true.

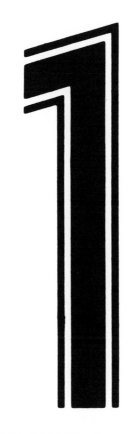

AEROBIC
DANCING

AEROBIC DANCING

Aerobic Dancing is a complete physical fitness program that *whispers* exercise and *shouts* fun. Whether performed at home with this book as your guide, or in one of my classes nationwide, it gives you the chance to dance freely in your own style, and at your own level. This is your opportunity to express—physically—your feelings about music by laughing, yelling, jumping, kicking, jogging, stretching, sliding, and swinging. And as you're entertaining yourself your body is going through a carefully-tested, well-monitored fitness workout that strengthens your heart and lungs, slims and trims your figure, and leaves you feeling exhilarated.

Unlike stop-start calisthenics and "spot" exercises designed for a particular part of the body, Aerobic Dancing is a *continuous* "get-it-all-together" activity. Instead of doing 10 repetitions of one exercise and 15 of another without any real benefit to the heart and lungs, you learn a variety of energetic, easy-to-remember dances—from Disco to the Charleston—that incorporate all the appropriate muscle-toning movements while developing your aerobic (cardiovascular) fitness. This fitness enables your body to process and deliver oxygen quickly and efficiently, and results in greater energy and vitality.

Aerobic Dancing recognizes the fact that, whatever benefits this program might promise, you most likely will not stick with it unless you are also *enjoying* yourself in the process. Therefore, skill and technique are not emphasized. This is a fitness sport that you play for *fun*, without worrying about *how* you look as you dance. Nor are you merely exercising to music, or performing a series of dance exercises—the most boring part of dancing classes. Instead, you are learning patterns that can be danced to suggested music, as well as complete dances that are choreographed emotionally to match the mood and beat of a particular song. It is this choreography that makes Aerobic Dancing a stimulating experience ("emotion in motion," as I like to call it) and why it will be easy for you to become a part of the music as you dance.

Drawing on the basic dance steps and patterns that I use in my classes, I've created a 12-week program for this book which can easily be expanded into a year-round program at home.

Aerobic Dancing can serve as your basic fitness conditioner, provided you follow my guidelines and set aside 30- to 45-minute sessions *at least* twice a week. If you really want to be physically fit, research has proved that vigorous exercise three times a week is necessary. This third workout, as I'll detail later (see p. 216), can be another session of Aerobic Dancing or any aerobic-type activity you enjoy, and which you're probably doing already: *i.e.* a long brisk walk, jogging, bicycling, rope skipping, swimming, racquetball, squash, tennis, etc.

I have to be honest with you: if you're out of shape, it will take time and continued participation for you to get into condition and stay that way. There's no effortless secret. You must huff, puff, and sweat in order for your body to get its proper all-around workout each week. But this doesn't mean that effective exercise has to be hard work or boring, or something you do just because it's good for you. Aerobic Dancing offers you a program that is active, challenging, creative, fun—and effective. You may not know it yet, but "playing" this fitness sport could be one of the best things that will ever happen to you. As one of our students has said, "Aerobic Dancing is almost a life necessity for me. I'm now beginning my fourth session and I feel beautiful through and through."

I want to get you *dancing* as soon as possible—in fact, the very first workout. But first I'll give some pertinent background about Aerobic Dancing and aerobic fitness, some appropriate cautions and suggestions to help maximize what you gain from the program, and a guide on how to use this book at home—either by yourself or, ideally, with friends and/or family members. Though most of my students across the country are women, we have a number of men as enthusiastic participants and instructors. Aerobic Dancing is also proving popular in school systems among both boys and girls. "Aerobic Dancing is one of many things that families can do together that can be fun and teach activity in a pleasurable way," says Dr. John L. Boyer, the Medical Director of the Exercise Laboratory and Adult Fitness Center at San Diego State University. "It is a wonderful way to get rhythmics, to get good cardiovascular endurance work, to become flexible, and to just be exuberant."

HOW AEROBIC DANCING BEGAN

I have always *loved* to dance, from the time I was six years old. My first solo came when I was eight—skipping rope to fast music while tap dancing—and although I was a generation too late with this vaudeville act, it gave me some important insights that I still use today.

An older girl in my dance group had this solo, but I was given the chance to replace her when she moved to another act. My dancing teacher told me, "You can have this solo, Jacki, because you skip rope pretty well. But you're huffing and puffing too much. If you're going to entertain the audience, you can't be breathless. You've got to tap and skip with a smile on your face."

I said, "Good, but how do I learn that?"

"Practice," she stressed.

So I got my rope out and I practiced jumping and tap dancing for hours at a time. And sure enough, it wasn't long before I could dance my solo and make it look easy, without breathing hard. My teacher called it "breath control"; today we know it as "physical conditioning."

I've been on a conditioning program ever since. But not until I was 26 years old did I discover how fit I actually was—solely as a result of my years of dancing—and how dance itself could be organized into an aerobic fitness program. This revelation came in 1969 when I was asked to host a television exercise program for the Air Force base in Puerto Rico where my husband was stationed. While preparing for the show, I studied the Air Force Aerobics program,

designed by Dr. Kenneth Cooper, and I took his famous 12-minute running test—a simple evaluation of a person's cardiovascular fitness based on how far the person can jog-run in 12 minutes. When I scored "excellent" on the test, even though I had never run before, I concluded that my years of dance training had not only kept my figure trim, but my heart and lungs in shape.

When the dances I choreographed for the television show drew favorable response, I decided to verify their physical benefits by setting up a research project involving Air Force wives. Using the 12-minute jog-run test as the basis for comparison, I found that a 12-week Aerobic Dancing program increased endurance as well as—and in most cases better than—a similar 12-week jogging program. Definite figure improvement was also noted.

After my husband and I moved to New Jersey in 1970, I kept refining and testing my dance routines until early 1971, when I decided to see what interest the public might have in such a program. Only six women ventured through the snow and ice to a church recreation room in South Orange, N.J., for my first Aerobic Dancing course. But by mid-March there were two courses of 25 each and I had started three other courses at a nearby YMCA. Aerobic Dancing, Inc. has since grown to over 50,000 students, is in nearly every state, and is expanding in foreign countries.

PHYSICAL AND PSYCHOLOGICAL BENEFITS OF AEROBIC DANCING

Early in every course of Aerobic Dancing, new students invariably come up to our instructors and talk about how much fun they're having, frequently saying, "I love it so much, it doesn't really seem like exercise. How can it possibly be good for me?" Our instructors know from experience that they can assure these newcomers they will soon see *and* feel definite figure and fitness benefits. Following are some of the benefits you, too, can expect from Aerobic Dancing:

1. In about six weeks you should notice a loss of unwanted inches off your figure and a firmer body. Each dance you learn is designed to tone and trim such common problem areas as the hips, thighs, waistline, and upper arms. Your legs

will look better than ever as the muscles become longer and leaner.

2. Aerobic Dancing is not intended as a weight reduction program, but when you increase your activity like this twice a week—while following a sound eating program—you're going to lose weight. You have three factors working on your behalf:

a. Your hunger is regulated. Although moderate exercise may increase hunger, as distinguished from appetite (which is psychological), vigorous aerobic exercise tends to decrease hunger physiologically by requiring blood to be "borrowed" from less active body systems, such as the stomach, and delivered to the more active skeletal muscle system. Until the blood supply is returned to your stomach, you will not have much of a desire for food. Even after the systems are again in balance, your hunger rarely increases more than normal.

b. Aerobic Dancing workouts are high calorie-burners because they demand a lot of energy. We have discovered that students burn about 300 calories in a moderate 45-minute class, which is equivalent to bicycling for 45 minutes at 7 mph. As many as 500 calories are burned during a vigorous 45-minute class, which compares to swimming for one hour at 30 yards/minute. Or look at it this way: if you weigh 117 pounds and watch television for 45 minutes, you burn approximately 75 calories.

c. Do you realize that when you exercise vigorously, you continue to burn more calories *following* the workout than you would during normal resting? For as long as six hours after a continuous 45-minute session of Aerobic Dancing, you can expect to burn about twice as many calories resting as you would if you had remained inactive.

3. By stressing continuous movement at a self-monitored level, Aerobic Dancing requires your body to demand increased amounts of oxygen over an extended period of time. The resulting aerobic fitness leads to the following benefits:

a. You are able to continue vigorous activities for a reasonably long period of time without becoming breathless or overly fatigued.

b. Your body recovers quickly from an active workout, whether it's Aerobic Dancing, racquetball, or jogging.

c. You have more daily energy as your body systems become more efficient. Instead of a "too tired to do anything" feeling, you develop a "joy of living" feeling.

d. Improved circulation allows muscles, skin, and vital organs to receive a better blood supply, which contributes to a healthier-looking complexion.

4. Aerobic Dancing may help prevent degenerative diseases by keeping the body systems in good working order and encouraging healthier habits. As one of my students has said, "I was motivated by Aerobic Dancing to give up smoking. I was smoking over two packs a day when I started the program."

5. You can develop increased flexibility, balance, coordination, body control, rhythm, and dancing ability. This improved physical ability—and accompanying self-confidence—will carry over into other sports and activities and make you more eager to try them.

6. This is a fitness program you can take along when you travel. Once you know some steps, you can dance to whatever music is available.

HOW AEROBIC DANCING WORKS

Later in this section I'll provide a suggested 12-week program, but first here's how each workout is organized, and then some important concepts and guidelines about Aerobic Dancing.

A SAMPLE WORKOUT

Flexibility: This opening segment involves eight stretching exercises done to suggested music, and should take 3½ to 4 minutes.

Warm-Up: A dance that starts out slowly with stretching and limbering movements that gradually increase your heart rate and prepare your body for the workout to come.

Aerobic Dancing Routines: A series of steps, patterns, and complete dances, styled to a wide range of music, that lasts about 15 to 30 minutes. The emphasis is on continuous motion, for this is the aerobic phase of your workout. During this time periodically take your working heart rate (WHR) to make sure that you stay within your WHR range.

Cool-Down: During this last 5 minutes, you perform a slow dance with gentle dance steps and walking patterns that allow your heart rate to return gradually to an acceptable recovery level. This is followed by the calf stretches you learned in the Flexibility routine.

LEARNING THE DANCES

None of my dances are designed for a specific proficiency level such as beginner, intermediate, or advanced. Instead, each one is intended to be as simple or as challenging as you want it to be. You first learn the basic steps and patterns for a dance, and the next option is yours: you can either do these patterns in any order you want, or you can dance them as they are choreographed to a specific piece of music.

STYLE AND SKILL

Aerobic Dancing is structured to ensure fitness and muscle tone, but I want you to "do your own thing" and feel the dances in your own way. How well you actually "dance" the steps, patterns, and Aerobic Dances is unimportant. Even in our classes the instructor has her back to the group as she leads them through a routine. This is an *individualized* program and you're successful at your own levels of fitness and skill.

ACTIVITY LEVELS

Every aspect of Aerobic Dancing is choreographed so that it can be performed at one or a combination of three activity levels—walking, jogging, or running—and still provide fitness benefits. "Walking" a pattern or dance means bouncing without lifting your feet very high and doing minimal arm movements. "Jogging" and "running" refer to how high you raise your knees and extend your arms. During every workout, you decide for yourself, using your working heart rate as a guide, when to exert yourself and when to ease off. If your activity level is too strenuous, use your arms less and walk the steps instead of jumping, jogging, or running.

CONTINUOUS RHYTHMIC MOVEMENT

Once you start each workout, *stay on your feet and always keep moving*. Remember, Aerobic Dancing is designed as continuous, rhythmic exercise, and in order to gain the desired aerobic benefits, you can't sit down between dances or stand and talk with your friends as you catch your breath. If you have to walk through all the routines in the beginning, don't worry.

THE "GET-IT-ALL-TOGETHER" CONCEPT

One of the drawbacks of most exercise programs is that they usually tackle just one of the three most important fitness requirements: either flexibility, muscle fitness, or aerobic fitness. This means that if your goal is to achieve all-around fitness, you must invest time and effort in more than one program. But the thing I hear most often is, "I don't have time."

Aerobic Dancing doesn't "waste" your time. By design, you're meeting all your important fitness needs in one workout. With over 600 muscles that need regular vigorous exercise, including your heart, why concentrate on only one group of muscles at a time when you can move your whole body at once and have fun doing it? In one dance pattern alone, you might be kicking your legs to the side to work on your inner and outer thighs, lifting your knees for the top of the back of your legs, swinging your arms for your waistline and upper arms, bouncing on your feet for your heart, and snapping your fingers—because it's FUN!

BEGINNING A PROGRAM OF AEROBIC DANCING

Aerobic Dancing is for *healthy* people who want to get fit and stay fit. If you are in good health, then aerobic exercise can and should become a part of your lifestyle, but it's important that you achieve this goal safely. Following are key precautions that I stress in my program:

First, inform your doctor and observe these guidelines:

UNDER 30: You can start exercising if you've had a checkup within the past year and the doctor found nothing wrong with you.

BETWEEN 30 AND 39: You should have a checkup within three months before you start exercising. The examination should include an electrocardiogram (EKG) taken at rest.

BETWEEN 40 AND 59: Same as for the 30–39 group with one important addition. Your doctor should also take an EKG to check your heart while you are exercising. (This is called a stress test.) Your pulse rate during this test should approach the level it would during aerobic workouts.

OVER 59: The same requirements as for the 40–59 age group except that the examination should be performed immediately before embarking on any exercise program.

CHECK YOUR WEIGHT

Obesity is a medical problem requiring modification of any vigorous physical exercise program, including Aerobic Dancing. If you're overweight you'll be placing unaccustomed stress on your hips, knees, and feet and you can easily elevate your heart rate to a dangerous level.

Assuming that you were not overweight in your early 20's your weight should not have increased more than 15 percent (e.g., if you weighed 120 at age 21, then you should not weigh more than 138 now). As a matter of interest, I'm including the following weight chart, which I use for my instructors and which I believe to be "ideal" weights.

WEIGHT Women	HEIGHT Feet	Inches	WEIGHT Men
85– 100	5	0	95– 110
90– 105	5	1	100– 115
95– 110	5	2	105– 121
100– 115	5	3	110– 126
105– 120	5	4	115– 132
110– 125	5	5	120– 137
115– 130	5	6	125– 143
120– 135	5	7	130– 148
125– 140	5	8	135– 154
130– 145	5	9	140– 159
135– 150	5	10	145– 165
140– 155	5	11	150– 170
145– 160	6	0	155– 176
150– 165	6	1	160– 181
155– 170	6	2	165– 187

HEART RATE MONITORING

Since I want to ensure the safety and effectiveness of every Aerobic Dancing workout, heart rate monitoring serves two important purposes.

First, it is a gauge by which you can assess the intensity of your workout at any point. By keeping your working heart rate (WHR) within your individual WHR range, you'll know that you are doing enough to derive benefit, and yet not so much as to be dangerous. Second, it is a motivational factor, allowing you to measure, objectively, your progress as you advance through the 12-week program.

There are three heart rates of interest in Aerobic Dancing, and each of them indicates something about your level of physical fitness.

Resting Heart Rate: Your resting heart rate (RHR) can be a fitness indicator because it tells you how hard your heart is working. A person in good aerobic condition usually has a lower resting heart rate than that of a person in poor aerobic condition. (The average RHR for women is 78-84 and for men 72-78.) If you are healthy, you may find that as you get involved in Aerobic Dancing, your resting heart rate decreases significantly, indicating that your heart has become stronger. By not having to contract so often, it can

WORKING HEART RATE RANGE

Beats per Minute (BPM)

*RHR	AGE 30 and under	31—40	41—50	51—60
50— 51	137— 195	131— 185	128— 180	125— 175
52— 53	138— 195	132— 185	129— 180	126— 175
54— 56	139— 195	133— 185	130— 180	127— 175
57— 58	140— 195	134— 185	131— 180	128— 175
59— 61	141— 195	135— 185	132— 180	129— 175
62— 63	142— 195	136— 185	133— 180	130— 175
64— 66	143— 195	137— 185	134— 180	131— 175
67— 68	144— 195	138— 185	135— 180	132— 175
69— 71	145— 195	139— 185	136— 180	133— 175
72— 73	146— 195	140— 185	137— 180	134— 175
74— 76	147— 195	141— 185	138— 180	135— 175
77— 78	148— 195	142— 185	139— 180	136— 175
79— 81	149— 195	143— 185	140— 180	137— 175
82— 83	150— 195	144— 185	141— 180	138— 175
84— 86	151— 195	145— 185	142— 180	139— 175
87— 88	152— 195	146— 185	143— 180	140— 175
89— 91	153— 195	147— 185	144— 180	141— 175

DO NOT EXCEED 140 BPM DURING
FIRST TWO WEEKS

*The ideal time to take your resting heart rate(RHR) is before you get out of bed in the morning. Otherwise, make sure you sit quietly for at least 15 minutes.

pump more blood with each contraction. This enables it to conserve energy as it does its daily work, and gives you more energy *all* day.

Working Heart Rate: The working heart rate is an excellent indicator of the intensity and the effectiveness of your workout. As exercise becomes more vigorous and more oxygen is required, the heart increases its rate of beating to supply oxygen to the muscles, and this in turn develops aerobic fitness.

Take your working heart rate *immediately* after each dance or after learning or practicing a pattern continuously for 3 to 5 minutes. Locate your pulse as quickly as possible and keep walking slowly as you count your heart beat for 6 seconds. Just add a zero to get your rate per minute, then check that this is within your individual WHR range. (See adjoining chart.) It is recommended that you stay within the *lower half* of your WHR range for the first 12 weeks. Thereafter you may work anywhere within your individual WHR range. *If your WHR is ever above your maximum rate, try a modified activity level for the remainder of your workout.*

No matter what your range might be, an additional safety factor is to *stay below 140* for the first two weeks of the program. For example, if you're a terrific memorizer and you want to learn all the dances in a three-day crash course, or you're a former dancer who smokes two packs a day and you haven't done any jumping around for two years, then you might be able to get into this program and quickly build up a very high working heart rate. *Don't take that risk.* Conversely, you may be surprised that your heart rate is not very high in the beginning. This is because you probably won't be working at a very high level of continuous exertion in the early learning process. So don't be thinking, "Gee, my heart rate isn't really getting up there." It will be high enough to be in your working heart range as soon as you've become familiar with some basic dance patterns.

Recovery Heart Rate: This measurement is taken 5 minutes after you've stopped exercising. Locate your pulse and count it for 15 seconds as you stand in place, then multiply this number by 4 to get your rate per minute. If the count is greater than 120, you know you're overextending yourself, so simply continue to walk slowly and stretch until the rate is 120 or less. Ten minutes after exercising it should be below 100. If not, it's a sign to cut back on the intensity with which you exercise. At your next workout, dance less vigorously by walking more steps and using your arms less energetically.

Aerobic Dancing usually improves your recovery heart rate. After several weeks you should find your heart returning to normal faster than when you began the program.

Taking Your Heart Rate: Three ways to take your heart rate, in order of preference, are (1) placing your index and middle fingers on the thumb side of your inner wrist, (2) placing these same fingers at your temple, and (3) placing your fingers gently at the carotid artery located on either side of the neck. This last method has proven to be the easiest for most students, but a few cautions apply: Don't press too hard or you'll impede the blood flow; don't press on both sides of your neck at the same time; if you feel a sudden drop in your heart rate remove your fingers immediately.

(NOTE: Working heart rates are taken for 6 seconds because they drop off fairly rapidly, and this provides a more accurate measure than a longer period. Conversely, resting and recovery heart rates are more constant, and are taken for 15 seconds to increase the accuracy of the measurement. For precise monitoring use a watch or clock with a second hand.)

Three Ways to Take Your Heart Rate.

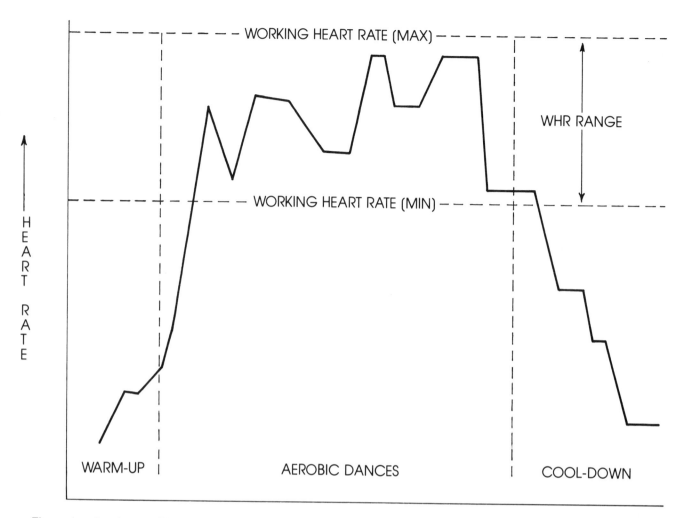

The chart above illustrates the heart rate changes that occur during a typical Aerobic Dancing workout. The minor changes in the "Aerobic Dances" phase are to be expected, and are a result of the slightly reduced demand between routines. (Adapted from Aerobic Dancing research by Lenore Zohman, M.D.)

MINIMIZING ACHES AND PAINS

You can't tackle any new physical exercise program without some aches and pains in the early learning stages, particularly if you've been leading a sedentary life. Even if you're a jogger or an active participant in sports, Aerobic Dancing will be using the same muscles but in a different way—and they may complain in the beginning. My objective is to help you *minimize* muscular discomfort and to keep you from doing too much too soon. If you can barely crawl out of bed the first couple of days, you may feel like a martyr—"Wow, this must really be good for me because I ache all over"—but that's not the kind of motivation I'm after. I want your body to *enjoy* Aerobic Dancing. Therefore, try to observe the following guidelines:

1. A wooden floor is the best surface for any kind of dancing, but a carpet is fine as long as you can move freely without tripping.

2. Whatever surface you use, remember always to wear shoes, as this is a jogging-type activity. An athletic shoe with good arch support and heel cushioning is essential. Tennis shoes, or shoes that are designed for both forward *and* lateral movement, are preferable to running or jogging shoes that are designed primarily for forward motion.

3. Any loose-fitting sports clothing or a leotard is fine. Support stockings and cotton sport socks are also recommended. Most students, both men and women, seem to prefer shorts and a tee shirt.

4. Learn to maintain proper body alignment. Although I encourage a "do-your-own-thing" approach when it comes to your dancing style and intensity level, I'm emphatic that you strive to maintain good posture. Keep reminding yourself to DANCE TALL, not only to allow your respiratory system to function effectively, but to avoid possible muscle strain and fatigue. For example, if you let your abdominal muscles hang loose when you dance, you could be straining lower back muscles. Or if you lean forward when you jog and kick your feet up behind you, you may strain the muscles of your shins and cause painful shin splints.

5. Try to move mainly on the front half of your feet, or even flat-footed. *Do not* dance high on the balls of your feet. Running or dancing on your toes may strain your Achilles tendon.

6. Remember to lift your knees a bit, as this will help your jogging form in addition to giving you a better aerobic workout.

7. Warm up properly and begin your activity gradually. Using my flexibility and warm-up routines will prepare your body for the vigorous dancing movements to follow.

8. *Always* include the cool-down routine at the end of your workout, and then do the calf stretches.

9. On the day following an Aerobic Dancing workout, do the flexibility routine to keep your muscles active and minimize possible soreness or stiffness. This is especially important in the beginning weeks. As your fitness level improves, try another aerobic activity between "dance days."

10. If you have a layoff, re-enter the program slowly.

BUILT-IN SAFEGUARDS

The Aerobic Dancing program offers important built-in safeguards. First of all, if you're out of shape the learning process gradually and gently tones your muscles and strengthens your cardiovascular system.

Second, if you're already in good shape from jogging or sports, following the learning progression I suggest will allow your muscles to adapt to being used in a different way.

Third, the movement progression in each workout from warm-up through cool-down is choreographed to be physiologically safe and sound.

Fourth, there's my activity levels concept. For example, you can begin dancing your way to fitness by walking through all the dance steps and patterns you are learning and practicing. Soon you'll be able to "jog" the dances by adding a little more bounce, "walking" steps or patterns only when you need to catch your breath. Gradually you'll find that you're dancing many sequences at the "running" level, only slowing down when necessary.

By adjusting and modifying your activity levels in this manner, you will *train* your body systems instead of straining them, making for a safer, more enjoyable experience.

OTHER HEALTH AND SAFETY HINTS

1. Refrain from eating a hearty meal immediately before exercising vigorously. Afterwards, do not consume more calories than you would under ordinary circumstances. The fact that you've worked hard may not offset the extra calories or justify a "reward," especially if you're interested in weight control.

2. Do not consume alcoholic beverages before your workout, since alcohol affects the coronary blood vessels. After participation, refrain from having any drinks for an hour or two, as they may go right to your head.

3. You should drink water as needed during your workout to prevent possible dehydration.

4. If you're a smoker, DO NOT SMOKE DURING YOUR WORKOUT. Smoking, in general, will inhibit your progress in Aerobic Dancing, but it is better to exercise vigorously and be a smoker if the alternative is to remain sedentary.

5. If you already have backache or other back problems before embarking on this program, describe the format to your doctor and then follow his or her advice. The doctor might suggest possible modifications.

6. If you're pregnant, consult your doctor.

HOW TO GET THE MOST FROM THIS BOOK

By buying this book you've shown you're a self-starter who's willing to spend some time reading, following instructions, and teaching yourself. As my part of the bargain, I've designed all the dances in this book to require a minimum effort on your part. The steps and patterns that comprise each dance are easy to understand, easy to follow, easy to memorize, and FUN to do.

This is because they involve natural, basic body movements that you probably did as a child. I'm not asking that you have special skills in order to master Aerobic Dancing.

With that in mind, here are some reminders as you set out to learn Aerobic Dancing:

1. *Be patient.* It takes approximately two weeks for most people to gain some confidence in Aerobic Dancing, and to feel comfortable about what they're trying to do. Take the attitude that you're learning a new sport. Few people expect to be able to play a tennis match after one or two lessons. The same holds true for Aerobic Dancing. You may feel like you're moving with two left feet at times, but as your body command improves from workout to workout, so will your coordination, balance, and endurance, allowing you to loosen up and move in more continuous rhythmic sequences.

2. *Avoid too much too soon.* You want your fitness to keep pace with your exertion level so that you will always feel great about each workout. In other words, as you gradually learn patterns that you eventually want to perform as a complete dance, you're gaining fitness that enables you to increase your activity level and become even more fit.

3. It is important that you develop the habit of *moving* at a level that's comfortable and safe for you, BUT KEEP MOVING at some level for 30-45 minutes.

4. When learning a new step, hold the book in front of you for easy reference.

5. In reviewing a step, my students find it helpful to say aloud what they want their feet to do. For example, they might say, "Step out, cross . . . step out, cross."

6. Learn the steps and patterns *without* music, but practice them with music.

7. Steps and patterns begin with your right foot.

8. Keep in mind that, for fun and fitness, it's not necessary for you always to begin or end on the correct foot or to do the steps the suggested number of times.

9. If you like, practice in front of a full-length mirror. Not necessarily to see if you're doing things *right*, but because this can make each workout more fun. You have another person to dance with and you see what the dances look like.

10. Treat this book as a *workbook*: feel free to write in it, adding notes, highlights, or reminders that help you through your workout.

11. Aerobic Dances are designed to be energetic, peppy, and spirited whether you perform them at a walking, jogging, or running level.

12. DANCE WITH A SMILE ON YOUR FACE.

TIMING YOUR WORKOUT

Once you know the dances and only need a brief review, I've allowed—as an ideal goal—just *one minute* between each Aerobic Dance and the next. During this time *keep moving* as you:

- take your 6-second working heart rate,
- take the record off the phonograph or change tapes,
- put on the next piece of music,
- briefly review the next dance.

Allowing this one minute between dances, here's how a 30-minute workout might be organized:

Flexibility routines and Warm-up dance . . .	8.00
Charleston	3.00
Hustle	3.30
Boogie	3.00
Rock	3.15
Cool-down dance and calf stretches	5.00

TOTAL TIME: 30.45

(Once you've memorized the dances and don't need to review them, you need only about 30 seconds between dances.)

You're probably thinking, "I can never be ready in one minute." Don't worry if it takes a little longer, so long as you're being as efficient as possible and not wasting time between dances. If you're tired and you need a breather, just walk through the next dance. Without this one-minute goal in mind, the tendency will be to take too much time between dances. Remember, your working heart rate drops rapidly once you finish a vigorous dance, and you want to keep it in your WHR range during the Aerobic Dancing phase of your workout.

GETTING YOURSELF ORGANIZED FOR EACH WORKOUT

Here are some pointers to help ensure the fewest number of delays in your workout:

1. Have your dance area cleared of any possible obstructions and designate the front of your dance space.

2. Review the workout plan to familiarize yourself with the steps and patterns learned in previous sessions.

3. Have this book lying open on the floor in front of you, or propped up on a table or chair, as an easy reference.

4. Before starting, review the music suggested for each dance in the workout and decide what you're going to play. (Use the music index p. 222.) Then pull the records out of their covers so they're ready to flip on your stereo. Or, get your tapes together and cue them up for the beginning of each song.

MEASURING YOUR PROGRESS

If you have at least two Aerobic Dancing workouts a week, 30 to 45 minutes each, you'll realize improvements in your aerobic fitness and muscle tone in several ways.

Heart rate monitoring and your increasing ability to work harder for longer periods of time will indicate your cardiovascular improvement. If you start out at a low fitness level, it will be easy to get your working heart rate into your WHR range. The concern, in fact, is that you not exceed the top of your recommended range. But once you've learned a couple of dances, your *average* WHR is likely to drop, even though you may be dancing at the same intensity level. This is because you're gaining in fitness, which means you are going to have to work harder in order to raise your WHR and keep it within your desired range. Now is the time to try dancing more energetically by lifting your knees a little higher and stepping out! *Also notice an important difference*: you can now work at a more intensive pace for a longer period of time because your heart has become more efficient.(Those of you who are already fit when you come into the program should probably strive to work at a jogging level from the very beginning and concentrate on moving your arms vigorously in order to raise your heart rate into your WHR range—and keep it there. But don't overlook the self-monitoring aspects built into the learning procedure, because you're using your muscles in a different way.)

Figure-toning progress will be self-evident by how you look. But again, one warning: *don't let the scales be the final judge,* for in many cases a loss of inches is noticed before you see any real change in actual weight. The reason is that you're turning fat weight into muscle weight, and muscle weight is heavier than fat weight. So you're going to *look* 100 percent better and *feel* 100 percent better, but because of this conversion of body tissue—especially if you started the program in poor physical shape—you won't see as drastic a change in your weight as you think you should.

THE AEROBIC DANCING PHILOSOPHY: HAVE FUN AND PLAY!

Aerobic Dancing is one of the most effective physical fitness programs because it has the necessary elements to prevent boredom and exercise dropouts. Many people are initially attracted by the promise that they're going to look better and feel better, but soon they become so involved in the fun and challenge of the activity that they almost forget they're benefiting from an aerobic conditioning program. They sign up for a second 12-week course, and a third and a fourth, because they find that Aerobic Dancing is a sport they play for the sheer enjoyment they gain *during the activity*. I feel this is the bottom line for a successful exercise program: participants *want* to continue with the program on a regular basis so that the fitness benefits they gain are sustained and not quickly lost through a return to inactivity.

Therefore, as you get into Aerobic Dancing, you'll realize that exercise doesn't have to be drudgery, done only for the final result. Exercise can be play, so draw out the carefree child that's inside you. It's boring to be an adult *all* the time! In Aerobic Dancing, we want you to feel free just to ham it up and even *pretend* that you're a Broadway dancer. Yes, pretend, because it's this freedom from examining *how* you do it that gives your body the chance just to swing in and try to do a dance naturally—to move without worry as to whether skill and technique are correct, or even improving. By taking this approach, you will discover that dance is so much more than you ever realized—and that an exercise program can be a happening that shouts fun!

THE 12-WEEK PROGRAM

In the middle section of this book, I'll be giving you 16 original Aerobic Dances, plus two Warm-up dances and two Cool-down dances. You can learn these dances and get in shape by working at your own pace or, ideally, by following my suggested 12-week program. Each of my workouts is carefully paced, contains optimal variety, covers basic muscle groups, and provides aerobic exercise of sufficient intensity and duration.

When you learn each dance, you'll start with the steps that comprise pattern one. After you memorize these steps and practice the suggested pattern, you can begin to learn the steps for the remaining patterns. Then, once you're familiar with the patterns, you're ready to put them all together and "dance the dance." You may want to start out by performing these patterns in any order you want, to suggested music, until you've danced approximately 2½-3 minutes. Once you're ready for more of a challenge you can learn one of the two chreographed routines given for each dance. The first routine for each dance is the easiest for most people to learn. Then the second routine can be used to continue your fitness program beyond the first 12 weeks. (See page 209.)

In learning the choreographed dances, you might find it helpful to imagine that you're following a recipe for a gourmet fitness treat. I give you all the ingredients—the different steps and patterns—and once you know them and practice them, all you have to do is follow my recipe. Your goal is to put these ingredients into a dance and come up with a smooth mixture that flows and makes you feel like a dancer.

Following is the 12-week progression you can use as you learn the Aerobic Dances in this book. Since we all learn at different speeds, I'm not asking you to follow these guidelines to the letter. If you're not able to finish what I suggest in two workouts every week, feel free to set aside a third day as your "catch-up" session. Or use this extra day to master the material covered in workouts one and two. When you organize your own workouts, my only concerns are (1) that you *always* include my Flexibility, Warm-up, and Cool-down routines, and (2) that you keep your working heart rate in your WHR range for at least 15 minutes.

In any event, whatever progression you follow, try to fit in a third aerobic workout each week.

YOUR FIRST 12-WEEK PROGRAM

WEEK ONE

Workout One*
1. Learn the eight Flexibility movements.
2. Learn Warm-up patterns one and two.
3. Learn Charleston pattern one. (WHR** as needed)
4. Cool down by doing Warm-up patterns one and two. (This helps you memorize the Warm-up patterns and gives you less new material to learn this first day—and for the first two weeks.)
5. Do 8 calf stretches. (RHR)

Workout Two
1. Flexibility routine.
2. Practice Warm-up patterns one and two, and learn patterns three and four.
3. Practice Charleston pattern one, and learn pattern two. (WHR as needed)
4. Cool down by doing all four Warm-up patterns.
5. Do 8 calf stretches. (RHR)

Workout Three
1. Repeat Workout Two,
    OR . . .
2. Try brisk walking.

Remember:
*Spend between 30 and 45 minutes on each workout.

**Take your Working Heart Rate (WHR) for 6 seconds after each Aerobic Dance and after each learning or practice segment that lasts 3 minutes. Take your Recovery Heart Rate (RHR) at the end of every workout. Note: RHR=Recovery Heart Rate, NOT Resting Heart Rate.

WEEK TWO

Workout One
1. Flexibility routine.
2. Practice the Warm-up patterns.
3. Learn Charleston pattern three. (WHR as needed)
4. Practice all three Charleston patterns. (WHR as needed)
5. Learn Hustle pattern one. (WHR as needed)
6. Cool down with the Warm-up patterns.
7. Calf stretches. (RHR)

Workout Two
1. Flexibility routine.
2. Practice Warm-up Dance. ("Higher and Higher")
3. Practice the Charleston Dance. ("Sweet, Sweet Smile"; WHR as needed)
4. Practice Hustle pattern one, and learn pattern two. (WHR as needed)
5. Cool down with Warm-up Dance.
6. Calf stretches. (RHR)

Workout Three
1. Repeat Workout Two,
    OR . . .
2. Try cycling.

WEEK THREE

NOTE:

Your goal for the next four weeks is to dance the equivalent of *four* Aerobic Dances per workout (this includes time spent practicing patterns) at your own level — repeating dances when necessary.

Workout One
1. Flexibility.
2. Warm-up Dance.
3. Learn Hustle pattern three. (WHR as needed)
4. Practice all three Hustle patterns. (WHR as needed)
5. Charleston Dance. (WHR)
6. Repeat Charleston Dance. (WHR)
7. Learn Cool-down patterns one and two.
8. Calf stretches. (RHR)

Workout Two
1. Flexibility.
2. Warm-up Dance.
3. Practice the Hustle Dance. ("Y.M.C.A."; WHR as needed)
4. Charleston Dance. (WHR)
5. Repeat Charleston Dance. (WHR)
6. Practice Cool-down patterns one and two, and learn patterns three and four.
7. Calf stretches. (RHR)

Workout Three
1. Repeat Workout Two, OR . . .
2. Try brisk walking.

WEEK FOUR

Workout One
1. Flexibility.
2. Warm-up Dance.
3. Charleston Dance. (WHR)
4. Repeat Charleston Dance. (WHR)
5. Hustle Dance. (WHR)
6. Repeat Hustle Dance. (WHR)
7. Learn Boogie pattern one.
8. Practice the Cool-down patterns.
9. Calf stretches. (RHR)

Workout Two
1. Flexibility.
2. Warm-up Dance. (Try to have it memorized by now.)
3. Charleston Dance. (WHR)
4. Hustle Dance. (WHR)
5. Repeat Hustle Dance. (WHR)
6. Practice Boogie pattern one, and learn pattern two. (WHR as needed)
7. Practice the Cool-down Dance. ("Hopelessly Devoted To You")
8. Calf stretches. (RHR)

Workout Three
1. Repeat Workout Two, OR . . .
2. Try cycling.

WEEK FIVE

Workout One
1. Flexibility.
2. Warm-up Dance.
3. Practice both Boogie patterns. (WHR as needed)
4. Learn Rock pattern one. (WHR as needed)
5. Charleston Dance. (WHR)
6. Hustle Dance. (WHR)
7. Cool-down Dance.
8. Calf stretches. (RHR)

Workout Two
1. Flexibility.
2. Warm-up Dance.
3. Practice the Boogie Dance. ("Jump Shout Boogie"; WHR as needed)
4. Practice Rock pattern one, and learn pattern two. (WHR as needed)
5. Charleston Dance. (WHR)
6. Hustle Dance. (WHR)
7. Cool-down Dance.
8. Calf stretches. (RHR)

Workout Three
1. Repeat Workout Two, OR . . .
2. Try swimming.

WEEK SIX

Workout One
1. Flexibility.
2. Warm-up Dance.
3. Practice Rock patterns one and two, and learn pattern three. (WHR as needed)
4. Learn Stretch pattern one. (WHR as needed)
5. Hustle Dance. (WHR)
6. Boogie Dance. (WHR)
7. Cool-down Dance.
8. Calf stretches. (RHR)

Workout Two
1. Flexibility.
2. Warm-up Dance.
3. Practice all three Rock patterns. (WHR as needed)
4. Practice Stretch pattern one, and learn pattern two. (WHR as needed)
5. Hustle Dance. (WHR)
6. Boogie Dance. (WHR)
7. Cool-down Dance.
8. Calf stretches. (RHR)

Workout Three
1. Repeat Workout Two, OR . . .
2. Try rope skipping.

WEEK SEVEN

> NOTE:
>
> Your goal for the next four weeks is to dance the equivalent of *six* Aerobic Dances per workout (this includes time spent practicing patterns) at your own level—repeating dances when necessary.

Workout One
1. Flexibility.
2. Warm-up Dance.
3. Practice the Rock Dance. ("Desirée"; WHR as needed)
4. Practice Stretch patterns one and two, and learn pattern three. (WHR as needed)
5. Learn Disco pattern one (WHR as needed)
6. DANCE SOME DANCES! Depending upon the time you have left over, and which dances you need to work on, just dance some dances you know. *But*, rotate these dances so you don't forget any, and take your WHR after each dance.
7. Cool-down Dance.
8. Calf stretches. (RHR)

Workout Two
1. Flexibility.
2. Warm-up Dance.
3. Practice all three Stretch patterns. (WHR as needed)
4. Practice Disco pattern one, and learn pattern two. (WHR as needed)
5. Rock Dance. (WHR)
6. DANCE SOME DANCES! (WHR after each dance)
7. Cool-down Dance.
8. Calf stretches. (RHR)

Workout Three
1. Repeat Workout Two,
    OR . . .
2. Try swimming.

WEEK EIGHT

Workout One
1. Flexibility.
2. Warm-up Dance.
3. Practice the Stretch Dance. ("Come Share My Love"; WHR as needed)
4. Practice Disco patterns one and two, and learn pattern three. (WHR as needed)
5. Learn Country pattern one. (WHR as needed)
6. DANCE SOME DANCES! (WHR after each dance).
7. Cool-down Dance.
8. Calf stretches. (RHR)

Workout Two
1. Flexibility.
2. Warm-up Dance.
3. Practice all three Disco patterns. (WHR after each dance)
4. Practice Country pattern one, and learn pattern two. (WHR as needed)
5. Stretch Dance (WHR)
6. DANCE SOME DANCE! (WHR after each dance)
7. Cool-down Dance. (Try to have it memorized by now.)
8. Calf stretches. (RHR)

Workout Three
1. Repeat Workout Two,
    OR . . .
2. Try rope skipping.

WEEK NINE

Workout One
1. Flexibility.
2. Warm-up Dance.
3. Practice the Disco Dance. ("Le Freak"; WHR as needed)
4. Practice Country patterns one and two, and learn pattern three. (WHR as needed)
5. Learn Broadway pattern one. (WHR as needed)
6. DANCE SOME DANCES! (WHR after each dance)
7. Cool-down Dance.
8. Calf stretches. (RHR)

Workout Two
1. Flexibility.
2. Warm-up Dance.
3. Practice all three Country patterns. (WHR as needed)
4. Practice Broadway pattern one, and learn pattern two. (WHR as needed)
5. Disco Dance. (WHR)
6. DANCE SOME DANCES! (WHR after each dance)
7. Cool-down Dance.
8. Calf stretches. (RHR)

Workout Three
1. Repeat Workout Two,
      OR . . .
2. Try jogging.

WEEK TEN

Workout One
1. Flexibility.
2. Warm-up Dance.
3. Practice the Country Dance. ("Stargazer"; WHR as needed)
4. Practice Broadway patterns one and two, and learn pattern three. (WHR as needed)
5. DANCE SOME DANCES! (WHR after each dance)
6. Cool-down Dance.
7. Calf Stretches. (RHR)

Workout Two
1. Flexibility.
2. Warm-up Dance.
3. Practice all three Broadway patterns. (WHR as needed)
4. Practice the Broadway Dance. ("One"; WHR as needed)
5. Country Dance. (WHR)
6. DANCE SOME DANCES! (WHR after each dance)
7. Cool-down Dance.
8. Calf stretches. (RHR)

Workout Three
1. Repeat Workout Two,
      OR . . .
2. Try racquetball or squash.

WEEK ELEVEN

> **NOTE:**
> Your goal from now on is to dance *eight* Aerobic Dances per workout—at your own level—repeating dances when necessary.

Workout One
1. Flexibility.
2. Warm-up Dance.
3. Memorize TWO Aerobic Dances. (WHR as needed)
4. Broadway Dance. (WHR)
5. DANCE SOME DANCES! (WHR after each dance)
6. Cool-down Dance.
7. Calf stretches. (RHR)

Workout Two
1. Flexibility.
2. Warm-up Dance.
3. Memorize TWO more Aerobic Dances (WHR as needed)
4. DANCE SOME DANCES! (WHR after each dance)
5. Cool-down Dance.
6. Calf stretches. (RHR)

Workout Three
1. Repeat Workout Two, OR . . .
2. Try jogging.

WEEK TWELVE

Workout One
1. Flexibility.
2. Warm-up Dance.
3. Memorize TWO more Aerobic Dances. (WHR as needed)
4. DANCE SOME DANCES! (WHR after each dance)
5. Cool-down Dance.
6. Calf stretches. (RHR)

Workout Two
1. Flexibility.
2. Warm-up Dance.
3. Memorize the LAST TWO Aerobic Dances. (WHR as needed)
4. DANCE SOME DANCES! (WHR after each dance)
5. Cool-down Dance.
6. Calf stretches. (RHR)

Workout Three
1. Repeat Workout Two, OR . . .
2. Try racquetball or squash.

DANCING!

FLEXIBILITY ROUTINE

The Flexibility routine gently prepares your body for vigorous aerobic activity by increasing the elasticity of your muscles and tendons, thereby helping to prevent strains. These exercises should take 3½ to 4 minutes— OR YOU'RE GOING TOO FAST. You might think, "I can do these exercises in one minute," but the object is to go *slowly* and make sure you stretch and limber your body.

These movements are not choreographed into patterns, because Flexibility isn't intended as a dance. However, I have listed music that provides the desired background. Do the Flexibility routine before every Aerobic Dancing workout so that eventually it becomes second nature to you. You'll find that this routine is also excellent to do before you participate in any active sport.

BODY TWISTS:
stretches back and sides of body

A. Begin with feet shoulder-width apart, arms hanging at sides.

B. Gently turn to the R and look behind you at the heel of your L foot (hands continue to hang and follow the gentle twist of the body).

C. Return to starting position and gently turn to the L side and look at heel of R foot.

FOOT CIRCLES:
stretches foot and ankle muscles

A. Begin with feet slightly apart and hands on hips.

B. Rotate R foot slowly outward, starting on inside of ball of foot. Put gentle pressure on foot. Reverse action to rotate inward. Repeat with L foot.

KNEE AND LOWER LEG CIRCLES:
stretches calf, knee, and ankle muscles

A. Begin with weight on L foot. If necessary, balance yourself by placing L hand on wall or chair.

B. Raise R knee and hold gently below knee with R hand. Rotate lower leg and foot outward. Reverse action to rotate inward. Repeat with L foot.

FLAMINGO FLINGS:
stretches front of thighs

A. Begin with weight on L foot. If necessary, balance yourself by placing L hand on wall or chair.

B. Lift R knee and hold leg between knee and ankle. Pull gently to the rear ending with R thigh in line with L leg. Hold for 8 counts. Repeat with L leg.

33

CALF STRETCHES:
stretches calf and ankle muscles

A. Begin with feet together.

B. Take a big step forward with R foot, bending R knee.
1. Keep L leg straight.
2. Keep both feet flat on floor and pointed forward.
3. Place both hands, arms straight, above L knee.
4. Hold 16 counts.

Repeat with L leg.

SIDEBENDS:
stretches sides of body and waist

A. Begin with feet in stride position and arms in jogging position.

B. Bend to the R side gently and smoothly and return to starting position. Repeat to the L.

A. Begin with feet shoulder-width apart and arms held out in front.

B. Slowly bend forward (4 counts) and down from the waist *as far as comfortable*, keeping knees relaxed. IT IS NOT NECESSARY TO TOUCH TOES OR FLOOR. Hold for 8 counts.

C. Stand up slowly (4 counts) *bending knees slightly* to take pressure off the lower back.

SPORTY STRETCH:
stretches inner thigh muscles of straight leg
and front of thigh of bent leg

A. Begin by standing with feet approximately 3 feet apart with L foot facing forward and R foot facing R diagonal.

B. Bend R knee, keeping weight even on both feet, and place hands, with elbows bent, above R knee. *Keep both feet flat on floor.* Hold 16 counts. Repeat, bending L knee.

SUGGESTED MUSIC:

"I Write The Songs" by *Barry Manilow*

"If You Know What I Mean" by *Neil Diamond*

"Just The Way You Are" by *Billy Joel*

"(Our Love) Don't Throw It All Away" by *Andy Gibb*

FLEXIBILITY
ROUTINE

1. Body Twists— 10, alternate R and L

2. Foot Circles— 4 outward R foot; 4 inward R foot
        — 4 outward L foot; 4 inward L foot

3. Knee and Lower
    Leg Circles— 4 outward R leg; 4 inward R leg
        — 4 outward L leg; 4 inward L leg

4. Flamingo Flings— R leg— 8 counts
        — L leg— 8 counts

5. Calf Stretches— R, L, R, L (16 counts each)

6. Sidebends— 8, alternate R and L (arms in jogging
    position)

7. Hamstring Stretch— 4 (16 counts each)

8. Sporty Stretch— R, L (16 counts each)

This routine should take between 3½ and 4 minutes.

THE WARM-UP!

A good warm-up routine is important to safe, healthy participation in any aerobic-type activity. Warming up raises the temperature of muscles to make it easier for energy-supplying chemical reactions to occur, and it gradually increases your heart rate. My warm-up routine for Aerobic Dancing also prepares you emotionally by getting you ready to really move out. This routine has simple movements and combinations with emphasis on a gradual progression. It's also activity-directed, which means that you practice skills you'll use in the dances rather than doing a series of general exercises.

SUGGESTED MUSIC

"Higher and Higher"
by *Rita Coolidge*

"How Deep Is Your Love"
by *The Bee Gees*

"There Will Be Love"
by *Lou Rawls*

"Mandy"
by *Barry Manilow*

SHOULDER ROLLS DOUBLE AND SINGLE

A. Begin with feet shoulder-width apart and arms hanging at sides.

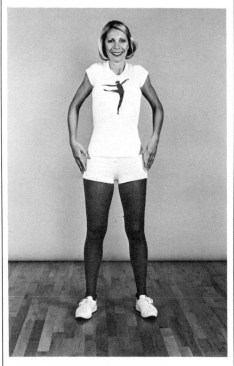

B. DOUBLE: Roll both shoulders up, back, down, and around in a continuous movement.

C. SINGLE: Roll R shoulder up, back, down, and around in a continuous movement. Roll L shoulder in same manner.

SIDEBENDS DOUBLE AND SINGLE

A. Begin with feet in stride position and arms overhead.

B. DOUBLE: Bend to the R, return to starting position, bend to the R *again*, then return to starting position. Repeat to the L.

C. SINGLE: Bend to the R dropping R arm; return to starting position. Bend to the L dropping L arm; return to starting position.

ADD SNAPS: Each time you bend and each time you return, snap your fingers.

KNEEBEND SWEEP SLOW

A. Begin with feet together and arms out at sides.

B. Bend your knees slightly as you sweep arms down and around — 4 COUNTS.

C. Straighten your knees as you stretch arms up and around — 4 COUNTS.

TWO-STEP PRESENT

A. Begin with feet together and arms down at sides.

B. RIGHT: Step R, Draw L foot to R. Step R, Draw L foot to R. As you do this, smoothly present R arm forward, around, and down to R side.

C. LEFT: Step L, Draw R foot to L. Step L, Draw R foot to L. As you do this, smoothly present L arm forward, around, and down to L side.

WARM-UP PATTERN ONE

Sidebends *Double* — R, L, R, L

    Arms: Both arms overhead.

               Snap 4 times for each *double* bend.

Sidebends *Single* — R, L, R, L

    Arms: One arm overhead, one arm down at side.

               Snap 2 times for each *single* bend.

Kneebend Sweep *Slow* — 2 (8 counts each)

Practice 1X

WARM-UP PATTERN TWO

Walk— 4 moving around the room

    Arms: Swing naturally in opposition.

Two-Step "Present"— R, L

    Arms: R arm presents around when moving R, and

              L arm presents around when moving L.

Practice 4X's

KNEEBEND SWEEP FAST

A. Begin with feet together and arms out at sides.

B. Bend your knees slightly as you sweep arms down around—2 COUNTS.

C. Straighten your knees as you stretch arms up and around—2 COUNTS.

KNEELIFTS

A. Begin with feet together and hands on hips.

B. Raise R knee, then return to starting position. Repeat with L knee.

WALK 'N' CLAP

Do 8 walks in a FULL CIRCLE to the R, lifting knees a bit. Clap hands in front of chest on each walk and lean slightly side to side.

FOUR-STEP

A. Begin with feet together and hands on hips.

B. RIGHT: Step to R with R foot.

C. Draw L foot to R foot. CONTINUE: Step R, Draw L foot to R; Step R, Draw L foot to R; Step R, Draw L foot to R.

D. LEFT: Reverse directions and do to the L.

LUNGE FORWARD

A. Begin with feet together and hands on hips.

B. Lunge Forward on R foot, bending both knees. Push arms forward.

C. Return to starting position. Pull arms in with a clap. Repeat with L foot.

WARM-UP PATTERN THREE

Kneebend Sweep *Fast* — 2 (4 counts each)

Kneelifts — R, L, R, L
   Arms: Hands on hips.

Walk 'n' Clap — 8 in a FULL CIRCLE R

                                   Practice 4X's

WARM-UP PATTERN FOUR

Four-Step— to the R

    Arms: Hands on hips.

Lunge Forward— 2 R foot

    Arms: Push-forward and pull-in with a clap for each lunge.

Four-Step— to the L

    Arms: Hands on hips.

Lunge Forward— 2 L foot

    Arms: Push-forward and pull-in with a clap for each lunge.

Practice 4X's

GET IT ALL TOGETHER—DANCE!

SUGGESTED MUSIC

"Higher and Higher" by *Rita Coolidge*

"How Deep Is Your Love" by *The Bee Gees*

"There Will Be Love" by *Lou Rawls*

"Mandy" by *Barry Manilow*

Shoulder Rolls Double— 6 fast

Raise Arms up to Overhead— 4 counts

PATTERN ONE

Sidebends *Double*— R, L, R, L

    Arms: Both arms overhead.

        Snap 4 times for each *double* bend.

Sidebends *Single*— R, L, R, L

    Arms: One arm overhead, one arm down at side.

        Snap 2 times for each *single* bend.

Kneebend Sweep *Slow*— 2 (8 counts each)

PATTERN TWO—4 times

Walk— 4 moving around the room

    Arms: Swing naturally in opposition.

Two-Step "Present"— R, L

    Arms: R arm presents around, then

        L arm presents around.

PATTERN THREE—4 times

Kneebend Sweep *Fast*—2 (4 counts each)

Kneelifts—R, L, R, L
    Arms: Hands on hips.

Walk 'n' Clap—8 in a FULL CIRCLE R

PATTERN FOUR—4 times

Four-Step—to the R
    Arms: Hands on hips.

Lunge Forward—2 R foot
    Arms: Push-forward and pull-in with a
       clap for each lunge.

Four-Step—to the L
    Arms: Hands on hips.

Lunge Forward—2 L foot
    Arms: Push-forward and pull-in with
       a clap for each lunge.

Shoulder Rolls Single —8

"HIGHER AND HIGHER"
(Rita Coolidge)

WARM-UP DANCE

> During singing stretch arms up and around—4 times slow
> Wait 4 counts (you'll hear 4 beats—this sets tempo)
> Shoulder Rolls Double—6 fast
> Raise Arms up to overhead—4 counts

Pattern ONE—*1 time*
  Sidebends *Double*—R, L, R, L (snap 4 times for each)
  Sidebends *Single*—R, L, R, L (snap 2 times for each)
  Kneebend Sweep *Slow*—2 (8 counts each)

Pattern TWO—*4 times* (move around the room and end where you began)
  Walk—4 (arms swing naturally in opposition)
  Two-Step "Present"—R, L

*Pattern THREE**—*2 times*
  Kneebend Sweep *Fast* —2 (4 counts each)
  Kneelifts—R, L, R, L (hands on hips)
  Walk 'n' Clap—8 in a FULL CIRCLE R

Pattern FOUR—*2 times*
  Four-Step—R (hands on hips)
  Lunge Forward—2 R foot (push-forward and pull-in with a clap for each lunge)
  Four-Step—L (hands on hips)
  Lunge Forward—2 L foot (push-forward and pull-in with a clap for each lunge)

THREE—*2 times*

FOUR—*2 times*

> Shoulder Rolls Single—8
> Kneebend Sweep Slow—2 (8 counts each; music fades)

Hint to help you stay with the music:
*The first two times you do this pattern there will be music with no vocal.

54

"HOW DEEP IS YOUR LOVE"
(Bee Gees)

WARM-UP DANCE

> Wait 8 counts (singing begins after these 8 counts—this sets tempo)
> Stretch arms up and around—1 (8 counts)
> Shoulder Rolls Double—6 fast
> Raise Arms up to overhead—4 counts

Pattern ONE—1 time
  Sidebends *Double*—R, L, R, L (snap 4 times for each)
  Sidebends *Single*—R, L, R, L (snap 2 times for each)
  Kneebend Sweep *Slow*—2 (8 counts each)

Pattern TWO—4 times (move around the room and end where you began)
  Walk—4 (arms swing naturally in opposition)
  Two-Step "Present"—R, L

Pattern THREE* —2 times
  Kneebend Sweep *Fast*—2 (4 counts each)
  Kneelifts—R, L, R, L (hands on hips)
  Walk 'n' Clap—8 in a FULL CIRCLE R

Pattern FOUR—2 times
  Four-Step—R (hands on hips)
  Lunge Forward—2 R foot (push-forward and pull-in with a clap for each lunge)
  Four-Step—L (hands on hips)
  Lunge Forward—2 L foot (push-forward and pull-in with a clap for each lunge)

THREE—2 times

FOUR—1 time

> Shoulder Rolls Single—8
> Kneebend Sweep Slow—2 (8 counts each; music fades)

Hint to help you stay with the music:
* The first time you do this pattern, the beginning lyrics are "and you
may not think I care for you." Begin Sweep on word "may."

THE CHARLESTON!

SUGGESTED MUSIC

"Sweet, Sweet Smile"
by *The Carpenters*

"Da Doo Ron Ron"
by *Shaun Cassidy*

"Southern Nights"
by *Glen Campbell*

YOUR FAVORITE CHARLESTON TUNE!

THE CHARLESTON!

A. Begin with feet together and arms in jogging position with palms forward.

B. *Touch* Forward with R foot as both arms swing to the R.

C. *Step* Back onto R foot as both arms swing to the L.

CHARLESTON WALK

A. Begin with feet together and arms in jogging position with palms forward.

B. *Step* Forward on R foot, HEEL FIRST as both arms swing to the R.

D. *Touch* Back with L foot as both arms swing to the R.

E. *Step* Forward onto L foot as both arms swing to the L.

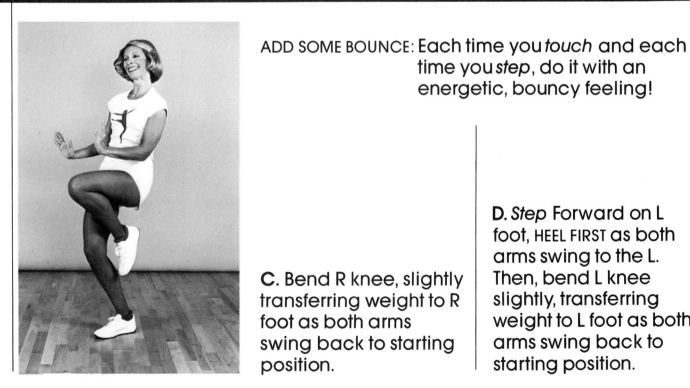

ADD SOME BOUNCE: Each time you *touch* and each time you *step*, do it with an energetic, bouncy feeling!

C. Bend R knee, slightly transferring weight to R foot as both arms swing back to starting position.

D. *Step* Forward on L foot, HEEL FIRST as both arms swing to the L. Then, bend L knee slightly, transferring weight to L foot as both arms swing back to starting position.

BENEFITS

- Legs
- Arms
- Waistline
- Hips
- Aerobic (Bouncing and Jogging)

FORM

- Keep your back straight on the Charleston!

- Gently twist upper body side to side on the Charleston Walk.

- Lift your knees slightly when you jog, and avoid landing high on balls of feet.

CHARLESTON PATTERN ONE

The Charleston!— 2

    Hint— Say this to yourself 2 times:

        "Touch-Forward, Step-Back, Touch-Back,

        Step-Forward"

    Arms: Swing both arms side to side.

Charleston Walk— 4 in a HALF CIRCLE R

    Arms: Swing both arms side to side.

Jog— 8 to finish the circle

    Arms: Jogging position.

                        Practice 2X's

                        Brief Rest

                        Practice 2X's

STEP-OUT, CROSS-OVER

A. Begin with feet together and arms in jogging position with palms forward.

B. *MOVING TO R: Step* R with R foot, lifting knee and swinging arms a bit to the R.

C. Lift L knee to step L foot *across* R foot while swinging arms a bit to the L. CONTINUE: Step-Out R, Cross-Over L, Step-Out R, Cross-Over L.

D. *MOVING TO L:* Begin with feet together. *Step* L with L foot, lifting knee and swinging arms a bit to the L. Lift R knee to step R foot *across* L foot while swinging arms a bit to the R. CONTINUE: Step-Out L, Cross-Over R, Step-Out L, Cross-Over R.

ADD SOME BOUNCE: Each time you *step* and each time you *cross* do it with an energetic, bouncy feeling!

A. Begin with feet together, knees relaxed, and arms in jogging position.

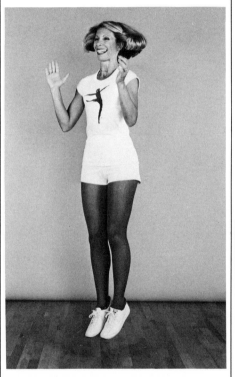

B. Jump upward with feet together and knees relaxed.

C. When feet land, clap hands in front of chest keeping knees relaxed, then add a small bounce.

BENEFITS

- Back of Thighs
- Hips
- Legs
- Aerobic (Bouncing)

FORM

- Try to keep upper body facing front on Step-Out, Cross-Over.

- Do with a "jive" feeling!

- Smile!!

CHARLESTON PATTERN TWO

Step-Out, Cross-Over— 3 moving to R
    Arms: Jogging position with palms forward and
        swing side to side a bit.

Break Slow— 2

Step-Out, Cross-Over— 3 moving to L
    Arms: Jogging position with palms
        forward and swing side to side a bit.

Break Slow— 2

           Practice 2X's
           Brief Rest
           Practice 2X's

KNEELIFTS HOPPING

A. Begin with feet together and arms in jogging position.

B. Hop on L foot as you lift R knee and gently slap knee with both hands. Bounce feet together.

C. Again, hop on L foot as you lift R knee and gently slap knee with both hands. Bounce feet together. Repeat A through C, lifting L knee and hopping on R foot.

HIT HEEL HOPPING

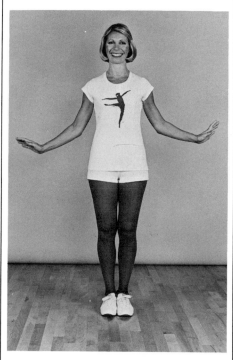

B. Hop on L foot as you kick up R heel to the rear and hit it with R hand.

A. Begin with feet together and arms in flipped 'V' position.

C. Bounce feet together.

D. Again, hop on L foot as you kick up R heel to the rear and hit it with R hand. Bounce feet together. Repeat A through D, kicking up L heel and hopping on R foot.

BENEFITS

- Back of Thighs
- Legs
- Arms
- Waistline
- Hips
- Aerobic (Hopping and Jogging)

FORM

- Keep your back straight as you lift your knees and hit your heels.

- Gently twist upper body side to side on the Charleston Walk.

- Lift your knees slightly when you jog backward.

CHARLESTON PATTERN THREE

Kneelifts Hopping—2 R knee

    Arms: Gently slap knee with both hands each time.

Hit Heel Hopping—2 R heel

    Arms: Both arms are in flipped 'V' position; hit

             heel with R hand each time.

Kneelifts Hopping—2 L knee

    Arms: Gently slap knee with both hands each time.

Hit Heel Hopping—2 L heel

    Arms: Both arms are in flipped 'V' position; hit

             heel with L hand each time.

Charleston Walk—4 forward

Jog Backward—6

    Arms: Jogging position.

JUMP FEET TOGETHER WITH A CLAP!

Practice 2X's

Brief Rest

Practice 2X's

GET IT ALL TOGETHER—DANCE!

THE CHARLESTON!

PATTERN ONE

The Charleston!—2

Hint— Say this to yourself 2 times:

"Touch-Forward, Step-Back, Touch-Back,

Step-Forward"

Arms: Swing both arms side to side.

Charleston Walk—4 in a HALF CIRCLE R

Arms: Swing both arms side to side.

Jog— 8 to finish the circle

Arms: Jogging position.

PATTERN TWO

Step-Out, Cross-Over— 3 moving to R

Arms: Jogging position with palms forward

and swing side to side a bit.

Break Slow— 2

Step-Out, Cross-Over— 3 moving to L

Arms: Jogging position with palms forward

and swing side to side a bit.

Break Slow— 2

PATTERN THREE

Kneelifts Hopping—2 R knee

    Arms: Gently slap knee with both hands each time.

Hit Heel Hopping—2 R heel

    Arms: Both arms are in flipped 'V' position; hit

            heel with R hand each time.

Kneelifts Hopping—2 L knee

    Arms: Gently slap knee with both hands each time.

Hit Heel Hopping—2 L heel

    Arms: Both arms are in flipped 'V' position; hit

            heel with L hand each time.

Charleston Walk—4 forward

    Arms: Swing both arms side to side.

Jog Backward—6

    Arms: Jogging position.

JUMP FEET TOGETHER WITH A CLAP!

Repeat these patterns to music, in any order you want,
until you've danced approximately 2½—3 minutes.
TAKE YOUR WORKING HEART RATE.

"SWEET, SWEET SMILE"
(The Carpenters)

AEROBIC DANCE— CHARLESTON

> Wait 16 fast counts
> *Jog in Three's— 4 times as follows:*
> Jog in place R, L, R (jogging arms)
> Pause 1 count with L knee up
> Jog in place L, R, L (jogging arms)
> Pause 1 count with R knee up

Pattern ONE— 2 times
  The Charleston!— 2
  Charleston Walk— 4 in a half circle R
  Jog— 8 to finish the circle (jogging arms)

Pattern TWO*— 2 times
  Step-Out, Cross-Over— 3 moving to R (arms close, palms out)
  Break Slow— 2
  Step-Out, Cross-Over— 3 moving to L (same arms)
  Break Slow— 2

ONE— 2 times

TWO— 2 times

Pattern THREE— 2 times
  Kneelifts Hopping— 2 R knee (hit knee each time)
  Hit Heel Hopping— 2 R heel (hit heel each time)
  Kneelifts Hopping— 2 L knee (hit knee each time)
  Hit Heel Hopping— 2 L heel (hit heel each time)
  Charleston Walk— 4 forward
  Jog Backward— 6 (jogging arms)
  JUMP FEET TOGETHER WITH A CLAP!

TWO— 2 times

THREE— 2 times

Hint to help you stay with the music:
**The beginning lyrics are "I got to know that
  you love me." Step-Out on word "know."*

"DA DOO RON RON"
(Shaun Cassidy)

AEROBIC DANCE—CHARLESTON

> Wait 8 counts
> *Jog in Three's —3 times as follows:*
> Jog in place R, L, R.
> Pause 1 count with L knee up
> Jog in place L, R, L.
> Pause 1 count with R knee up

Pattern ONE—2 times
  The Charleston!—2
  Charleston Walk—4 in a half circle R
  Jog—8 to finish the circle (jogging arms)

> Break Slow—4*

Pattern TWO—2 times
  Step-Out, Cross-Over—3 moving to R (arms close, palms out)
  Break Slow—2
  Step-Out, Cross-Over—3 moving to L (same arms)
  Break Slow—2

> Jog—8 in a FULL CIRCLE R (jogging arms)

Pattern THREE—2 times
  Kneelifts Hopping—2 R knee (hit knee each time)
  Hit Heel Hopping—2 R heel (hit heel each time)
  Kneelifts Hopping—2 L knee (hit knee each time)
  Hit Heel Hopping—2 L heel (hit heel each time)
  Charleston Walk—4 forward
  Jog Backward—6 (jogging arms)
  JUMP FEET TOGETHER WITH A CLAP!

ONE—1 time

> Break Slow—4

TWO—1 time

THREE—2 times
  (Music fades.)

Hint to help you stay with the music:
*During these Breaks there will be music with no vocal.

THE HUSTLE!

SUGGESTED MUSIC

"You Should Be Dancing"
by the *Bee Gees*

"Y.M.C.A."
by the *Village People*

"It's a Miracle"
by *Barry Manilow*

"You Make Lovin' Fun"
by *Fleetwood Mac*

LUNGE SIDE

A. Begin with feet together and arms in jogging position

B. RIGHT: Lunge to the R with R leg, bending both knees and shooting arms overhead. Return to starting position, pulling arms in.

C. LEFT: Lunge to the L with L leg, bending both knees and shooting arms down. Return to starting position, pulling arms in.

A. Begin with feet together and arms in jogging position.

B. FORWARD: Jog forward 3, beginning with R foot.

C. Hop on R foot, lifting L knee high as you clap.

D. BACK: Jog back 3, beginning with L foot. Then hop on L foot, lifting R knee high as you clap.

BENEFITS

- Inner Thighs
- Outer Thighs
- Waistline
- Arms
- Back of Thighs
- Aerobic (Jogging)

FORM

- When you lunge side, keep toes pointed forward.

- Lift your knees slightly when you jog, and avoid landing high on balls of feet.

HUSTLE PATTERN ONE

Lunge Side— 8 (alternate R and L)
   Arms: Shoot-up, pull-in

              Shoot-down, pull-in

              for every 2 lunges

Hustle Jog— Forward, Back, Forward, Back
   Arms: Jogging position,

              Clap on each hop

Practice 2X's

Brief Rest

Practice 2X's

FOUR-STEP "CLAP"

A. Begin with feet together and arms in jogging position.

B. RIGHT: Step to R with R foot.

C. Draw L foot to R foot. CONTINUE: Step R, draw L foot to R; step R, draw L foot to R.

TWO-STEP "CLAP"

A. Begin with feet together and arms in jogging position.

B. RIGHT: Step R, draw L foot to R; step R, draw L foot to R as you clap hands.

C. LEFT: Step L, draw R foot to L; step L, draw R foot to L as you clap hands.

D. Step R, draw L foot to R foot as you clap hands.

E. LEFT: Step L, draw R foot to L;
　　　step L, draw R foot to L;
　　　step L, draw R foot to L;
　　　step L, draw R foot to L as you clap hands.

BENEFITS

- Legs
- Aerobic (Brisk Walking)

FORM

- This is a great pattern for concentrating on proper body alignment.

- Get the "feel" of the music!

- SMILE!!

HUSTLE PATTERN TWO

Four-Step "Clap"— R, L (8 counts each).
   Arms: Jogging position and
            clap on each 8th count.

Two-Step "Clap"— R, L, R, L (4 counts each).
   Arms: Jogging position and
            clap on each 4th count.

Practice 4 X's

SCISSOR DOUBLES

A. Begin with feet together and arms in jogging position.

B. RIGHT: Jump and land on both feet with R foot forward and L foot back, and knees relaxed.
Bounce once in this position.

C. LEFT: Jump and land on both feet, changing position so L foot is forward and R foot is back with knees relaxed.
Bounce once in this position.

ADD SNAPS: Each time you jump and each time you bounce, snap your fingers.

A. Begin with feet together, L hand on hip and R arm in jogging position.

B. Jump lightly to stride position with feet spread shoulder-width apart.

C. Jump feet together lightly to return to starting position.

ADD TWIRLS: Each time you jump, twirl R hand inward.

KNEELIFTS HOPPING

A. Begin with feet together and arms in jogging position.

B. RIGHT: Hop on L foot as you raise R knee.

C. Bounce feet together.

D. LEFT: Hop on R foot as you raise L knee. Then, bounce feet together.

ADD SNAPS: Each time you hop and each time you bounce, snap your fingers.

A. Begin with feet together, knees relaxed, and arms in jogging position.

B. Jump upward with feet together and knees relaxed.

C. When feet land, clap hands in front of chest, keeping knees relaxed. Then, ADD A SMALL BOUNCE.

BENEFITS

- Legs
- Back of Thighs
- Aerobic (Jumping and Hopping)

FORM

- Don't lean forward on Scissor Doubles.

- Always *land* with heels *only slightly* off the floor.

- Avoid landing high on balls of feet.

- Pretend you're doing an Aerobic Hustle at a Disco!

HUSTLE PATTERN THREE

Scissor Doubles— R, L, R, L
    Arms: Jogging position.
        Snap twice for each one.

Jumping Jack— 4
    Arms: L hand on hip; R twirls 4 times
        inward in jogging position.

Kneelifts Hopping— 6 (alternate R, L)
    Arms: Jogging position.
        Snap once for each one.

Break Slow— 2

Practice 2X's
Brief Rest
Practice 2X's

THE HUSTLE!

SUGGESTED MUSIC

"You Should Be Dancing" by the *Bee Gees*

"Y.M.C.A." by the *Village People*

"It's a Miracle" by *Barry Manilow*

"You Make Lovin' Fun" by *Fleetwood Mac*

PATTERN ONE

Lunge Side— 8 (alternate R and L)

Arms: Shoot-up, pull-in
Shoot-down, pull-in for
every 2 lunges.

Hustle Jog— Forward, Back, Forward, Back

Arms: Jogging position,
Clap on each hop.

PATTERN TWO

Four-Step "Clap"— R, L (8 counts each)

Arms: Jogging position and
Clap on each 8th count.

Two-Step "Clap"— R, L, R, L (4 counts each)

Arms: Jogging position and
Clap on each 4th count.

PATTERN THREE

Scissor Doubles— R, L, R, L

Arms: Jogging position,
Snap twice for each one.

Jumping Jack— 4

Arms: L hand on hip, R twirls 4 times inward
in jogging position.

Kneelifts Hopping— 6 (alternate R, L)

Arms: Jogging position,
Snap once for each one.

Break Slow— 2

**Repeat these patterns to music in any order
you want, until you've danced 3-3½ minutes.
TAKE YOUR WORKING HEART RATE.**

"YOU SHOULD BE DANCING"

(Bee Gees)

AEROBIC DANCE— HUSTLE

> Wait 8 counts
> Four-Step "Clap"— R, L (8 counts each)
> Two-Step "Clap"— R, L (4 counts each)

Pattern ONE* —1 time
  Lunge Side— 8, alternate R and L (shoot-up, pull-in, shoot-down, pull-in for every 2)
  Hustle Jog— Forward, Back, Forward, Back (clap on each hop)

Pattern TWO —1 time
  Four-Step "Clap"— R, L, (8 counts each)
  Two-Step "Clap"— R, L, R, L (4 counts each)

ONE —1 time

TWO —2 times

Pattern THREE ** —1 time
  Scissor Doubles— R, L, R, L (snap 8 times)
  Jumping Jack— 4 (L hand on hip, R twirls 4 times)
  Kneelifts Hopping —6, alternate R and L and try turning in a full circle R (snap 6 times)
  Break Slow— 2

> Hustle Jog— Forward, Back, Forward, Back

ONE— 1 times

THREE —2 times

TWO —1 time

THREE —2 times (there will be extra music, but end dance here and take WHR)

Hints to help you stay with the music:
*Vocal begins with this pattern.
**During this pattern there will be music with no vocal.

"Y. M.C.A."

(Village People)

AEROBIC DANCE — HUSTLE

> Wait 8 counts
> Four-Step "Clap" — R, L (8 counts each)
> Two-Step "Clap" — R, L (4 counts each)
> Four-Step "Clap" — R, L (8 counts each)
> Two-Step "Clap" — R, L (4 counts each)

Pattern ONE — 1 time
  Lunge Side — 8, alternate R and L (shoot-up, pull-in, shoot-down, pull-in for every 2)
  Hustle Jog — Forward, Back, Forward, Back (clap on each hop)

Pattern TWO — 1 time
  Four-Step "Clap" — R,L, (8 counts each)
  Two-Step "Clap" — R, L, R, L (4 counts each)

> Jog — 8 in a FULL CIRCLE R (jogging arms)

Pattern THREE* — 2 times
  Scissor Doubles — R, L, R, L (snap 8 times)
  Jumping Jack — 4 (L hand on hip, R twirls 4 times)
  Kneelifts Hopping — 6, alternate R and L and try turning in a full circle R (snap 6 times)
  Break Slow — 2

ONE — 1 time

TWO — 1 time

> Jog — 8 in a FULL CIRCLE R (jogging arms)

THREE — 2 times

ONE — 1 time

TWO — 1 time

> Jog — 8 in a FULL CIRCLE R (jogging arms)

THREE — 2 times (there will be extra music, but end dance here and take WHR)

Hint to help you stay with the music:
*Every time you do this pattern the beginning lyrics are "Y.M.C.A."

THE BOOGIE!

SUGGESTED MUSIC

"Jump Shout Boogie"
by *Barry Manilow*

"Johnny B. Goode"
by *John Denver*

"Rock 'n Roll Party Queen"
from the movie *Grease*

"In the Mood"
by *Ray Conniff*

TOUCH-SIDE, CROSS-OVER

A. Begin with feet together and arms in jogging position.

B. *Touch* R foot to R side as arms swing out at sides.

C. Step R foot *across* in front of L foot as arms swing downward to cross in front of chest.

D. *Touch* L foot to L side as arms swing out at sides. Step L foot *across* in front of R foot as arms swing downward to cross in front of chest.

ADD SOME BOUNCE: Each time you *touch* and each time you *cross*, do it with a lively, bouncy feeling!

BOOGIE JOG

A. Begin with feet together and arms at sides of waist, closed in loose fists with index fingers pointing down.

B. Jog Back with R foot as R arm extends down at R side and L hand moves up to side of chest.

C. Jog Back with L foot with L arm extending down at L side as R hand moves up to side of chest.

D. Do 4 more Boogie Jogs, then JUMP FEET TOGETHER WITH A CLAP!

BENEFITS

- Thighs
- Hips
- Arms
- Waistline
- Aerobic (Bouncing and Jogging)

FORM

- Swing arms energetically on Touch-Side, Cross-Over.

- Each time you *touch* and each time you *cross* ADD SOME BOUNCE!

- Lift your knees slightly when you jog backward, and avoid landing high on balls of feet.

BOOGIE PATTERN ONE

Touch-Side, Cross-Over— 6 moving FORWARD
(alternate R and L)
    Arms: Swing arms out at sides, then swing
        downward to cross in front of chest.

Boogie Jog— 6 moving BACKWARD

JUMP FEET TOGETHER WITH A CLAP!

                    Practice 3X's
                    Brief Rest
                    Practice 3X's

SEVEN-UP

A. Begin with feet together and arms in jogging position.

B. MOVING TO LEFT: Jog R foot over L foot.

C. Jog to L side with L foot.

D. Jog R foot over L foot; Jog to L side with L foot; Jog R foot over L foot; Jog to L side with L foot.

E. Jog R foot over L foot, then *kick* foot out to L side as you snap fingers.

F. MOVING TO RIGHT: Repeat A through E, beginning by jogging L foot over R foot.

HINT—Say: "1, 2, 3, 4, 5, 6, 7, UP!"

ROCK THREE, HOP

A. Begin with feet together and weight on L foot.

B. Rock to R foot with R knee slightly bent and L leg extended to L side.

C. Rock to L foot with L knee slightly bent and R leg extended to R side.

D. Rock to R foot with R knee slightly bent and L leg extended to L side, then HOP on R foot as you snap fingers.

E. Repeat A through D, beginning by rocking to L foot.

SWING STEP

A. Begin with feet together, weight on L foot, and hands on hips.

D. Swing R foot *back* and rock back on it as arms push-forward.

B. Step forward, heel first, transferring weight to R foot.

C. Step back, toe first, transferring weight to L foot.

E. Rock forward onto L foot as arms pull-in.

F. Rock back on R foot as arms push-forward. Rock forward onto L foot as arms pull-in.

HINT: Say: "Forward, back, rock, rock, rock, rock."

BREAK COMBO

A. Begin with feet together, knees relaxed, and arms in jogging position.

B. Do 2 *slow* Breaks *with* the small bounce.

C. Do 3 *fast* Breaks *without* the small bounce.

BENEFITS

- Inner Thighs
- Outer Thighs
- Legs
- Arms
- Aerobic (Jogging, Rocking, and Bouncing)

FORM

- Try to keep upper body facing front on Seven-Up.

- Keep back straight on Rock Three, Hop.

- Get in the "Spirit" of this dance with the Swing Step!

- Smile!!

BOOGIE PATTERN TWO

Seven-Up—L, R, L, R

   Arms: Jogging position and snap fingers at
           end of each one.

Rock Three, Hop—6

   Arms: Jogging position and snap fingers at
           end of each one.

Break Combo—1

   Arms: 2 slow claps, 3 fast claps.

Swing Step—4

   Arms: Hands on hips, then push-forward, pull-in,
           push-forward, pull-in, for each one.

Practice 1X

Brief Rest

Practice 1X

THE BOOGIE!

SUGGESTED MUSIC

"Jump Shout Boogie" by *Barry Manilow*

"Johnny B. Goode" by *John Denver*

"Rock 'n Roll Party Queen" from the movie *Grease*

"In the Mood" by *Ray Conniff*

PATTERN ONE

Touch-Side, Cross-Over— 6 moving FORWARD
(alternate R and L)
Arms: Swing arms out at sides, then swing
downward to cross in front of chest.

Boogie Jog— 6 moving BACKWARD

JUMP FEET TOGETHER WITH A CLAP!

PATTERN TWO

Seven-Up—L, R, L, R
    Arms: Jogging position and snap fingers at
            end of each one.

Rock Three, Hop—6
    Arms: Jogging position and snap fingers at
            end of each one.

Break Combo—1
    Arms: 2 slow claps, 3 fast claps.

Swing Step—4
    Arms: Hands on hips then push-forward, pull-in,
            push-forward, pull-in, for each one.

**Repeat these patterns to music, in any order you want,
until you've danced approximately 2½– 3 minutes.
TAKE YOUR WORKING HEART RATE.**

"JUMP SHOUT BOOGIE"
(Barry Manilow)

AEROBIC DANCE—BOOGIE

> Wait 16 fast counts
> Swing Step—4 (hands on hips then
>   push-forward, pull-in, push-forward,
>   pull-in for each one)

Pattern ONE—2 times
>   Touch-Side, Cross-Over—6 moving *forward*, alternate R and L (arms swing out at
>   sides, then swing downward to cross in front for each one)
>   Boogie Jog—6 moving *backward*
>   JUMP FEET TOGETHER WITH A CLAP!

Pattern TWO*—1 time
>   Seven-Up—L, R, L, R (jogging arms, snap at end of each one)
>   Rock Three, Hop—6 (jogging arms, snap at end of each one)
>   Break Combo—1

> Swing Step—4 (same arms)

ONE—2 times

TWO—1 time

> Swing Step—2 (same arms)

ONE—2 times

TWO—1 time

> Break Combo—1 (try turning in a full
>   circle R)

(Music fades)

Hint to help you stay with the music:
*The first and second time you do this pattern the beginning lyrics are "Jump, Shout."

"JOHNNY B. GOODE"
(John Denver)

AEROBIC DANCE — BOOGIE

> Wait 16 fast counts
> Rock Three, Hop— 6 (jogging arms, snap
>   at end of each one)
> Break Combo— 1

Pattern ONE— 2 times
  Touch-Side, Cross-Over— *4 moving forward*, alternate R and L (arms swing out at
    sides, then swing downward to cross in front for each one)
  Boogie Jog— 6 moving *backward*
  JUMP FEET TOGETHER WITH A CLAP!

Pattern TWO*— 1 time
  Seven-Up— L, R, L, R (jogging arms, snap at end of each one)
  Rock Three, Hop— 2 (jogging arms, snap at end of each one)
  Break Combo— 1

ONE — 2 times

TWO — 1 time

> Swing Step— 6, Try doing the last 4
>   turning in a full circle R (hands on
>   hips, then push-forward, pull-in,
>   push-forward, pull-in for each one)

ONE — 2 times

TWO — 1 time

> Swing Step— 6, Try doing the last 4
>   turning in a full circle R (same arms)

TWO — 1 time (there will be one extra beat plus vague music)

Hint to help you stay with the music:
*Every time you do this pattern the beginning lyrics are "Go, Go Johnny Go."

ROCK!

SUGGESTED MUSIC

"Desirée"
by *Neil Diamond*

"Don't Stop"
by *Fleetwood Mac*

"Love Will Keep Us Together"
by *The Captain and Tennille*

"That's When The Music Takes Me"
by *Neil Sedaka*

THIGH ROCKS DOUBLE

A. Begin with feet in stride position, knees flexed, and arms in jogging position.

B. Energetically shift weight to R foot, keeping L foot on floor.

C. Bounce once in this position.

D. Energetically shift weight to L foot, keeping R foot on floor.

E. Bounce once in this position.

A. Begin with feet together, knees relaxed, and arms in jogging position.

B. Jump upward with feet together and knees relaxed.

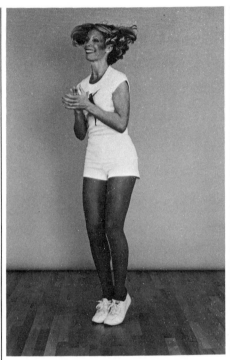

C. When feet land, clap hands in front of chest, keeping knees relaxed. Then, add a small bounce.

KNEELIFTS HOPPING— IN A FULL CIRCLE "LEFT"

A. Begin with feet together, knees relaxed, and arms in jogging position.

B. Hop on L foot, *raising R knee, turning to "LEFT" wall*, and snapping fingers. Bounce feet together.

C. Hop on R foot raising L knee, turning to rear, and snapping fingers. Bounce feet together. Do 2 more Kneelifts Hopping to end facing front.

CROSS, ROCK, STEP-TOGETHER-STEP
(follow photos R to L across top, and L to R across bottom).

F. Quickly *step* to R with R Foot.

E. Quickly jump L foot next to R foot ("*together*").

D. Face front and *step* to R with R foot with arms in jogging position.

G. *Cross* L foot over R foot so body and foot are facing R wall. R arm in jogging position and L arm pushes toward R Wall.

H. *Rock* back onto R foot.

114

A. Begin with feet together and arms in jogging position.

B. *Cross* R foot over L foot so body and foot are facing L wall. L arm in jogging position and R arm pushes toward L wall.

C. *Rock* back onto L foot.

I. Face front and *step* to L with L foot, with arms in jogging position.

J. Quickly jump R foot next to L foot ("*together*").

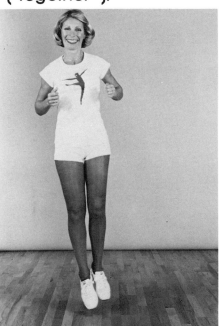

K. Quickly *step* to L with L foot.
HINT— Say "Cross, Rock, 1-2-3."

BENEFITS

- Inner Thighs
- Outer Thighs
- Legs
- Arms
- Back of Thighs
- Aerobic (Bouncing, Jumping, and Hopping)

FORM

- Look side to side on Thigh Rock Doubles.

- Keep back straight on Cross, Rock, Step-Together-Step.

- Remember to turn in a FULL CIRCLE *LEFT* on the Kneelifts Hopping.

ROCK PATTERN ONE

Thigh Rocks Double— 6
   Arm: Move arms vigorously
      in jogging position.

Break Slow— 2

                              Practice 2X's

ROCK PATTERN TWO

Cross, Rock, Step-Together-Step— 6 (alternate to L
      wall and to R wall)
   Arms: Single Arm Push, then
      jogging position.

Kneelifts Hopping— 4, alternate R and L, in a FULL
            CIRCLE *LEFT*
   Arms: Jogging position and snap on each
      Kneelift Hopping.

                              Practice 2X's
                              Brief Rest
                              Practice 2X's

HIGH WALK

A. Begin with feet together and arms hanging down at sides.

B. Walk with "pep" by lifting knees slightly and landing on balls of feet with a bouncy feeling. Arms swing in opposition.

TWO-STEP "SHOOT-UP"

A. Begin with feet together and arms in jogging position.

B. *RIGHT:* Step R as arms "Shoot-Up." Draw L foot to R foot as arms pull-in. CONTINUE: Step R as arms "Shoot-Up." Draw L foot to R foot as arms pull-in.

C. *LEFT:* Reverse direction and do to L.

TOM JONES STEP

A. Begin with feet together, arms in jogging position, and knees flexed. *Keep knees flexed throughout step.*

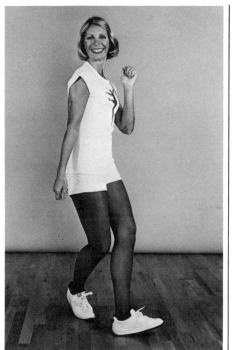

B. Step back with *R foot* as you roll back to L heel facing L diagonal, and drop R arm down to side (L arm in high jogging position).

C. Step back with *L foot* as you roll back to R heel facing R diagonal, and drop L arm down to side (R arm returns to high jogging position).

D. CONTINUE: Step back with *R foot*, dropping R arm (L arm returns to high jogging position); Step back with *L foot*, dropping L arm (R arm returns to high jogging position).

BENEFITS

- Legs
- Arms
- Waistline
- Aerobic (Brisk Walking and Bouncing)

FORM

- Really extend your arms and look up a bit on Two-Step "Shoot-Up."

- Do the Tom Jones Step as a continuous, smooth motion, and with a "Rock" feeling!

ROCK PATTERN THREE

High Walk—4 forward

    Arms: Swing arms in opposition.

Two-Step "Shoot-Up"—R, L, R, L

    Arms: Shoot arms up and pull-in

              twice for each one.

Tom Jones Step—R, L, R, L moving backward fast

    Arms: Begin in jogging position;

              drop R arm, drop L arm

              returning R arm, drop R arm

              returning L arm, drop L arm

              returning R arm.

Break Slow—2

                           Practice 4X's

GET IT ALL TOGETHER—DANCE

SUGGESTED MUSIC

"**Desirée**"
by *Neil Diamond*

"**Don't Stop**"
by *Fleetwood Mac*

"**Love Will Keep Us Together**"
by *The Captain and Tennille*

"**That's When The Music Takes Me**"
by *Neil Sedaka*

PATTERN ONE—2 TIMES

Thigh Rocks Double—6
   Arms: Move arms vigorously
      in jogging position.

Break Slow—2

PATTERN TWO

Cross, Rock, Step-Together-Step—6
   (alternate to L wall and to R wall)
   Arms: Single Arm Push, then jogging position.

Kneelifts Hopping—4, alternate R and L, in a FULL
   CIRCLE *LEFT*
   Arms: jogging position and snap
      on each Kneelift Hopping.

PATTERN THREE

High Walk— 4 forward

    Arms: Swing arms in opposition.

Two-Step "Shoot-Up"— R, L, R, L

    Arms: Shoot arms up and pull-in
              twice for each one.

Tom Jones Step— R, L, R, L moving backward **fast**

    Arms: Begin in jogging position;
           drop R arm, drop L arm
           returning R arm, drop R arm
           returning L arm, drop L arm
           returning R arm.

Break Slow— 2

**Repeat these patterns to music, in any order you want,
until you've danced approximately 2½—3 minutes.
TAKE YOUR WORKING HEART RATE.**

"DESIRÉE"
(Neil Diamond)

AEROBIC DANCE—ROCK

```
┌─────────────────────────────────────┐
│                                     │
│            Wait 8 counts            │
│                                     │
└─────────────────────────────────────┘
```

Pattern ONE—1 time
    Thigh Rocks Double—10
    Break Slow—2

Pattern TWO*—2 times
    Cross, Rock, Step-Together-Step—6 (single arm push, then jogging arms; 4 counts
                  each)
    Kneelifts Hopping—4, alternate R, L, in a FULL CIRCLE *LEFT* (jogging arms, snap 4 times)

Pattern ONE—1 time
    Thigh Rocks Double—2
    Break Slow—2

Pattern THREE**—2 times
    High Walk—4 forward (arms swing in opposition)
    Two-Step "Shoot-Up"—R, L, R, L
    Tom Jones Step—R, L, R, L, moving backward fast
    Break Slow—2

Pattern ONE—1 time
    Thigh Rocks Double—6
    Break Slow—2

TWO—2 times

Pattern ONE—1 time
    Thigh Rocks Double—2
    Break Slow—2

THREE—2 times

TWO—1 time

Pattern ONE—1 time
    Thigh Rocks Double—6
    Break Slow—2
    (Music fades)

Hints to help you stay with the music:
  *Vocal begins with this pattern.
  **When you do this pattern the beginning lyric will be "Desirée."

"DON'T STOP"
(Fleetwood Mac)

AEROBIC DANCE— ROCK

Wait 8 counts

Pattern ONE—1 time
　　Thigh Rocks Double— 10
　　Break Slow— 2

Pattern TWO*—2 times
　　Cross, Rock, Step-Together-Step— 6 (single arm push, then jogging arms; 4 counts
　　　　　　　　　　　　　　　　　　each)
　　Kneelifts Hopping— 4, alternate R, L, in a FULL CIRCLE *LEFT* (jogging arms, snap 4 times)

Pattern ONE—1 time
　　Thigh Rocks Double— 6
　　Break Slow— 2

Pattern THREE—2 times
　　High Walk— 4 forward (arms swing in opposition)
　　Two-Step "Shoot-Up"— R, L, R, L
　　Tom Jones Step— R, L, R, L, moving backward fast
　　Break Slow— 2

Pattern ONE—1 time
　　Thigh Rocks Double— 2
　　Break Slow— 2

TWO—1 time

Pattern ONE—1 time
　　Thigh Rocks Double— 2
　　Break Slow— 2

TWO—1 time

THREE—2 times

TWO—1 time

Pattern ONE—1 time
　　Thigh Rocks Double— 6
　　Break Slow— 2
　　(Music fades)

Hint to help you stay with the music:
*Vocal begins with this pattern.

THE STRETCH!

SUGGESTED MUSIC

"Come Share My Love"
by *Debbie Boone*

"Beautiful Music"
by *Barry Manilow*

"Everlasting Love"
by *Andy Gibb*

"Wayward Wind"
by *Crystal Gayle*

STRETCH-AROUND SWAYS

A. Begin with feet in stride position and hands in front of chest with elbows out at sides.

B. *TO THE R:* Bend R knee and sway to the R, as you do a breast stroke with both arms.

C. Sway back to the L and bend L knee, as you complete the breast stroke and end with hands in front of chest with elbows out at sides.

D. *TO THE L:* Bend L knee and sway to the L, as you do a breast stroke with both arms. Then, sway back to the R and bend R knee, as you complete the breast stroke and end with hands in front of chest with elbows out at sides.

LUNGE FORWARD "PRESENT"

A. Begin with feet together and arms in jogging position.

B. *RIGHT:* Lunge forward on R foot, bending both knees and presenting arms forward.

C. Return R foot next to L foot, pulling arms in.

D. *LEFT:* Lunge forward on L foot, bending both knees, and presenting arms forward. Return L foot next to R foot, pulling arms in.

ROCKING FOUNTAIN

A. Begin with feet together, facing R diagonal, and arms in jogging position.

B. *Right Diagonal:* Rock forward to R foot with R knee flexed and L leg extended back. Arms begin to fountain.

C. Rock back to L foot with L knee flexed and R leg extended forward. Arms continue to fountain up.

F. Rock forward to R foot again. Arms continue to fountain *down* at sides.

D. Rock forward to R foot again. Arms are at top of fountain.

E. Rock back to L foot again. Arms begin to fountain *down* at sides.

G. Rock back to L foot again. Arms continue to fountain *down* at sides.

H. JUMP FEET TOGETHER WITH A CLAP!

I. *Left Diagonal:* Repeat this sequence beginning with feet together, facing L diagonal, and start by rocking forward to *L* foot.

BENEFITS

- Thighs
- Legs
- Waistline
- Arms
- Back of thighs
- Aerobic (Rocking and Jumping)

FORM

- On Stretch-Around Sways really "lean-into" and "pull-away" from each one.

- Really "stretch" the fountain arms as you look up a bit and smile!

STRETCH PATTERN ONE

Stretch-Around Sways—*3 to the R*

    Arms: Do a complete breast stroke for each one.

Lunge Forward "Present"– R foot

    Arms: Present arms forward and pull-in.

Stretch-Around Sways—*3 to the L*

    Arms: Do a complete breast stroke for each one.

Lunge Forward "Present"– L foot

    Arms: Present arms forward and pull-in.   Practice 2X's

    Brief Rest

    Practice 2X's

STRETCH PATTERN TWO

Rocking Fountain– 6 rocks *to R diagonal* (R foot forward)

    Arms: Fountain arms up, around, and down once.
JUMP FEET TOGETHER WITH A CLAP!

Rocking Fountain– 6 rocks *to L diagonal* (L foot forward)

    Arms: Fountain arms up, around, and down once.
JUMP FEET TOGETHER WITH A CLAP!

    Practice 2X's

    Brief Rest

    Practice 2X's

JOG "STRETCH"

A. Begin with feet together and arms out at sides.

B. Jog 8 forward, stretching arms down, up, and around ONCE, slowly.

BREAK SLOW—2 in a HALF CIRCLE R

A. Begin with feet together, knees relaxed, and arms in jogging position.

B. Jump upward with feet together, knees relaxed, and turning in a ¼ circle R.

C. Land at ¼ circle point with knees relaxed and clapping hands, then add a small bounce.

D. Jump upward again turning in a ¼ circle R. Land at ½ circle point with knees relaxed and clapping hands. Then, add a small bounce.

BREAK COMBO—MOVING BACKWARD

A. Begin with feet together, knees relaxed, and arms in jogging position.

B. Do 2 *slow* Breaks *with* the small bounce, moving slightly backward.

C. Do 3 fast Breaks, without the small bounce, moving slightly backward.

BENEFITS

- Legs
- Thighs
- Hips
- Waistline
- Arms
- Aerobic (Jogging and Bouncing)

FORMS

- Lift your knees slightly when you jog, and avoid landing high on balls of feet.

- Really "Stretch" your arms down, up, and around on the Jog "Stretch" with a happy feeling!

STRETCH PATTERN THREE

Jog—4 forward
  Arms: Jogging position.

Break Slow—2 in a HALF CIRCLE R to face *rear*

Jog—4 to rear
  Arms: Jogging position.

Break Slow—2 in a HALF CIRCLE R to face *front*

Jog "Stretch"—8 forward
  Arms: Stretch down, up, and around.

Break Combo—1 moving backward
  Arms: 2 slow claps, 3 fast claps.

Practice 2X's
Brief Rest
Practice 2X's

GET IT ALL TOGETHER—DANCE!

SUGGESTED MUSIC

"Come Share My Love" by *Debbie Boone*
"Beautiful Music" by *Barry Manilow*
"Everlasting Love" by *Andy Gibb*
"Wayward Wind" by *Crystal Gayle*

PATTERN ONE

Stretch-Around Sways—*3 to the R*

    Arms: Do a complete breast stroke for each one.

Lunge Forward "Present"—R foot

    Arms: Present arms forward and pull-in.

Stretch-Around Sways—*3 to the L*

    Arms: Do a complete breast stroke for each one.

Lunge Forward "Present"—L foot

    Arms: Present arms forward and pull-in.

PATTERN TWO—2 TIMES

Rocking Fountain— 6 rocks *to R diagonal* (R foot forward)

    Arms: Fountain arms up, around, and down once.

JUMP FEET TOGETHER WITH A CLAP!

Rocking Fountain— 6 rocks *to L diagonal* (L foot forward)

    Arms: Fountain arms up, around, and down once.

JUMP FEET TOGETHER WITH A CLAP!

PATTERN THREE

Jog—4 forward
   Arms: Jogging position.

Break Slow—2 in a HALF CIRCLE R to face *rear*

Jog—4 to rear
   Arms: Jogging position.

Break Slow—2 in a HALF CIRCLE R to face *front*

Jog "Stretch"—8 forward
   Arms: Stretch down, up, and around.

Break Combo—1 moving backward
   Arms: 2 slow claps, 3 fast claps.

Repeat these patterns to music, in any order you want,
until you've danced approximately 3 — 3½ minutes.
TAKE YOUR WORKING HEART RATE.

"COME SHARE MY LOVE"
(Debbie Boone)

AEROBIC DANCE—STRETCH

```
┌─────────────────────────────────────┐
│                                      │
│            Wait 16 counts            │
│                                      │
└─────────────────────────────────────┘
```

Pattern ONE* —2 times
   Stretch-Around Sways— 3 *to the R*
   Lunge Forward "Present"— R foot
   Stretch-Around Sways— 3 *to the L*
   Lunge Forward "Present"—L foot

Pattern TWO** —2 times
   Rocking Fountain— 6 Rocks *to R diagonal* with R foot forward
   JUMP FEET TOGETHER WITH A CLAP!
   Rocking Fountain— 6 Rocks *to L diagonal* with L foot forward
   JUMP FEET TOGETHER WITH A CLAP!

Pattern THREE —1 time
   Jog— 4 forward (jogging arms)
   Break Slow— 2 in a HALF CIRCLE R
   Jog— 4 to rear (jogging arms)
   Break Slow— 2 in a HALF CIRCLE R
   Jog "Stretch"— 8 forward (really STRETCH arms down, up, and around one time)
   Break Combo—1 moving backward

ONE, TWO, and THREE exactly as written 2 MORE TIMES

TWO —2 times

THREE —1 time (music fades during Break Combo)

Hints to help you stay with the music:
 * Vocal begins with this pattern.
*** The beginning lyrics are "Come share my love." Begin
   rocking on word "love."*

"BEAUTIFUL MUSIC"
(Barry Manilow)

AEROBIC DANCE — STRETCH

Wait 16 counts

Pattern ONE* —1 time
   Stretch-Around Sways— 3 *to the R*
   Lunge Forward "Present"– R foot
   Stretch-Around Sways— 3 *to the L*
   Lunge Forward "Present"– L foot

Jog— 8 in a FULL CIRCLE R (jogging arms) Break Combo—1

ONE —1 time, THEN Jog —8 in a FULL CIRCLE R (jogging arms); Break Combo —1

Pattern TWO** —2 times
   Rocking Fountain— 6 Rocks *to R diagonal* with R foot forward
   JUMP FEET TOGETHER WITH A CLAP!
   Rocking Fountain— 6 Rocks *to L diagonal* with L foot forward
   JUMP FEET TOGETHER WITH A CLAP!

Jog— 8 in a FULL CIRCLE R (jogging arms)

TWO —2 times, THEN Break Combo —1 (try turning this Break Combo in a full circle R)

Pattern THREE —1 time
   Jog— 4 forward (jogging arms)
   Break— 2 slow in a HALF CIRCLE R
   Jog— 4 to rear (jogging arms)
   Break— 2 slow in a HALF CIRCLE R
   Jog "Stretch"– 8 forward (really STRETCH arms down, up, and around one time)
   Break Combo— 1 moving backward

Jog— 8 in a FULL CIRCLE R (jogging arms)

ONE —1 time, THEN jog —8 in a FULL CIRCLE R (jogging arms); Break Combo —1
TWO —2 times, THEN jog —8 in a FULL CIRCLE R (jogging arms)
TWO —2 times, THEN Break Combo —1 (try turning this Break Combo in a full circle R)
THREE —1 time
ONE —2 times, THEN Break Combo —1
(there will be extra music, but end dance here and take WHR)

Hints to help you stay with the music:
   * Vocal begins with this pattern.
   ** The beginning lyrics are "And when I heard." Begin rocking on word "heard."

DISCO!

SUGGESTED MUSIC

"Le Freak"
by *Chic*

"Disco Inferno"
by *The Trammps*

"Last Dance"
by *Donna Summer*

"New York City Rhythm"
by *Barry Manilow*

DISCO LUNGE SIDE

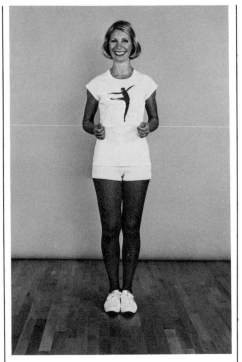

A. Begin with feet together and arms in jogging position.

B. RIGHT: Lunge to the R with R leg, bending both knees, as L arm shoots straight up, pointing, and R arm shoots straight down, pointing. Return to starting position, pulling arms in.

C. LEFT: Lunge to the L with L leg, bending both knees, as R arm shoots straight up, pointing, and L arm shoots straight down, pointing. Return to starting position, pulling arms in.

HUSTLE JOG

A. Begin with feet together and arms in jogging position.

B. FORWARD: Jog forward 3 beginning with R foot.

C. Hop on R foot, lifting L knee high as you clap.

D. BACK: Jog back 3 beginning with L foot. Then, hop on L foot, lifting R knee high as you clap.

DISCO JOG THREE, KICK

A. Begin with feet together and arms in jogging position.

B. Jog 3 in place, R, L, R, with subtle shoulder rolls forward R, L, R.

C. Kick L foot low to L side as you hop lightly on R foot and snap fingers.

D. Repeat beginning with L foot.

BREAK SLOW—4 IN A FULL CIRCLE R

A. Begin with feet together, knees relaxed, and arms in jogging position.

B. Jump upward with feet together, knees relaxed, and begin turning in a circle R.

C. Land with knees relaxed and clapping hands, then add a small bounce. Do three more "Breaks" to finish the circle.

BENEFITS

- Inner Thighs
- Outer Thighs
- Waistline
- Arms
- Back of Thighs
- Aerobic (Jogging)

FORM

- When you Disco Lunge Side, keep toes pointed forward.

- Lift your knees slightly when you jog, and avoid landing high on balls of feet.

- Dance these patterns with a "Travolta" style!

DISCO PATTERN ONE

Disco Lunge Side—R, L, R, L

    Arms: When lunging R, L arm points up and R
            arm points down. Pull arms into jogging
            position. Reverse arms when lunging L.

Hustle Jog—Forward, Back

    Arms: Jogging position, clap on each hop!

> Practice 2X's
> Brief Rest
> Practice 2X's

DISCO PATTERN TWO

Disco Jog Three, Kick—6

    Arms: Jogging position with subtle, alternate
            shoulder rolling action. Snap at end of
            each one.

Break Slow—4 in a FULL CIRCLE R

> Practice 2X's
> Brief Rest
> Practice 2X's

WIND-UP BOUNCE

A. Begin with feet in stride position, knees relaxed, with R hand on hip and L arm held out to L side.

B. Drop L arm in front of body and continue circling upward.

C. Complete circle, reaching arm overhead and around to starting position.

C. Continue to swing arms out to R side with knees bent, and end with a snap.

D. Reverse direction and swing to the L.

D. Do 2½ *more* wind-ups and end with both hands snapping to R side with elbows bent.

E. Reverse direction and wind-up R arm.

ADD BOUNCES: Each time you drop arm, circle arm and end with snap, bounce feet.

SWING 'N' SNAP

B. Swing both arms down with knees bent.

A. Begin with feet in stride position, knees relaxed, with arms to L side with elbows slightly bent.

BENEFITS

- Arms

- Waistline

- Thighs

- Legs

- Aerobic (Bouncing)

FORM

- Keep your back
  straight on the
  Wind-up Bounce.

- Make sure your
  knees are bent on
  Swing 'n' Snap.

- Really "feel the
  beat" and "get into"
  this dance!

DISCO PATTERN THREE

Wind-up Bounce— 3½ L arm, then snap (8 counts)
    Arms: R hand is on hip as L arm winds up. End
              with both arms to R with elbows bent,
              and snap.

Wind-up Bounce— 3½ R arm, then snap (8 counts)
    Arms: L hand is on hip as R arm winds up. End
              with both arms to L with elbows bent,
              and snap.

Swing 'n' Snap— 4 (8 counts)
    Arms: Swing arms down and out to the R, L, R, L.
              End each swing with a snap.

Break Slow— 4 in a FULL CIRCLE R

                              Practice 2X's
                              Brief Rest
                              Practice 2X's

GET IT ALL TOGETHER—DANCE!

SUGGESTED MUSIC

"Le Freak" by *Chic*

"Disco Inferno" by *The Trammps*

"Last Dance" by *Donna Summer*

"New York City Rhythm" by *Barry Manilow*

PATTERN ONE— 2 TIMES

Disco Lunge Side—R, L, R, L

    Arms: When lunging R, L arm points up and R
        arm points down. Pull arms into jogging
        position. Reverse arms when lunging L.

Hustle Jog—Forward, Back

    Arms: Jogging position, clap on each hop!

PATTERN TWO

Disco Jog Three, Kick—6

    Arms: Jogging position with subtle, alternate
        shoulder rolling action. Snap at end of
        each one.

Break Slow—4 in a FULL CIRCLE R

PATTERN THREE

Wind-up Bounce— 3½ L arm, then snap (8 counts)

    Arms: R hand is on hip as L arm winds up. End
            with both arms to R with elbows bent,
            and snap.

Wind-up Bounce— 3½ R arm, then snap (8 counts)

    Arms: L hand is on hip as R arm winds up. End
            with both arms to L with elbows bent,
            and snap.

Swing 'n' Snap—4 (8 counts)

    Arms: Swing arms down and out to the R, L, R, L.
            End each swing with a snap.

Break Slow—4 in a FULL CIRCLE R

**Repeat these patterns to music, in any order you want,
until you've danced approximately 3— 3½ minutes.
TAKE YOUR WORKING HEART RATE.**

"LE FREAK"
(Chic)

> Begin almost immediately, after first Ahhh . . .
> Disco Jog Three, Kick—6 (snap at end of each one)
> Break Slow—4 in a FULL CIRCLE R

Pattern ONE—2 times
   Disco Lunge Side—R, L, R, L
   Hustle Jog— Forward, Back (clap on hop)

Pattern TWO*—1 time
   Disco Jog Three, Kick—6 (snap at end of each one)
   Break Slow—4 in a FULL CIRCLE R

Pattern THREE—1 time
   Wind-up Bounce—3½ L arm, then snap (8 counts)
   Wind-up Bounce—3½ R arm, then snap (8 counts)
   Swing 'n' Snap—4
   Break Slow—4 in a FULL CIRCLE R

ONE—4 times

TWO—1 time

THREE—1 time

ONE—4 times

TWO—1 time

THREE—1 time

ONE—2 times (there will be extra music, but end dance here and take WHR)

Hint to help you stay with the music:
*The beginning lyrics will be "Have you heard."

"DISCO INFERNO"

(The Trammps)

AEROBIC DANCE—DISCO

```
┌─────────────────────────────────────┐
│                                      │
│           After Cymbal Crash,        │
│           Wait 8 counts              │
│                                      │
└─────────────────────────────────────┘
```

Pattern TWO—1 time
    Disco Jog Three, Kick—6 (snap at end of each one)
    Break Slow—4 in a FULL CIRCLE R

Pattern THREE—1 time
    Wind-up Bounce—3½ L arm, then snap (8 counts)
    Wind-up Bounce—3½ R arm, then snap (8 counts)
    Swing 'n' Snap—4
    Break Slow—4 in a FULL CIRCLE R

Pattern ONE*—2 times
    Disco Lunge Side—R, L, R, L
    Hustle Jog—Forward, Back (clap on hop)

TWO—1 time

THREE—1 time

ONE—2 times

TWO—1 time

THREE—1 time

ONE—4 times, THEN *Disco Lunge Side— R, L*

TWO—1 time

THREE—1 time

*ONE—4 times (there will be extra music, but end dance here and
take WHR)*

Hint to help you stay with the music:
*The beginning lyrics will be "Burn baby burn."

COUNTRY!

SUGGESTED MUSIC

"Stargazer"
by *Neil Diamond*

"Let Me Be There"
by *Olivia Newton-John*

"Walk Right Back"
by *Ann Murray*

"Sunflower"
by *Glen Campbell*

COUNTRY HOP

A. Begin with feet together and arms in jogging position.

D. Lightly jump feet to stride position as both arms swing to L side.

B. Lightly jump feet to stride position as both arms swing to R side.

C. Hop on R foot while placing L foot behind R calf. Snap fingers at R side.

COUNTRY JOG

A. Begin with feet together. Bend elbows with arms in at waist and hands at shoulder level.

E. Hop on L foot while placing R foot behind L calf. Snap fingers at L side.

B. Jog forward with R foot, leaning upper body to the R.

C. Jog forward L foot leaning upper body to the L.

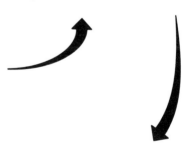

D. Do 2 more Country Jogs forward, then try 4 moving backward.

GUITAR THIGH ROCKS

A. Begin in stride position with knees flexed and arms positioned to play a guitar.

D. Energetically shift weight to L foot, keeping R foot on floor and strumming the guitar once.

B. *Doubles:* Energetically shift weight to R foot, keeping L foot on floor and strumming the guitar once.

C. Bounce once in this position strumming the guitar once.

BREAK COMBO

A. Begin with feet together, knees relaxed, and arms in jogging position.

B. Do 2 *slow* Breaks *with* the small bounce.

C. Do 3 *fast* Breaks *without* the small bounce.

E. Bounce once in this position strumming the guitar once.

F. *Singles:* Energetically shift weight to R foot as before, then immediately shift weight to L foot. Strum the guitar each time you shift weight.

BENEFITS

- Legs
- Arms
- Waistline
- Inner Thighs
- Outer Thighs
- Aerobic (Hopping, Jogging, and Bouncing)

FORM

- When jumping to stride on Country Hop, place weight evenly on both feet with heels close to floor.

- Make sure to lean side to side on Country Jogs, lift your knees slightly, and avoid landing high on balls of feet.

- Have fun strumming your guitar!

COUNTRY PATTERN ONE

Country Hop— R, L, R, L

    Arms: Swing both arms side to side with a
            snap.

Country Jog— 4 forward

            —4 backward

    Arms: Bend elbows with arms in at waist and
            hands at shoulder level, then lean side
            to side as you jog.

Practice 2X's

Brief Rest

Practice 2X's

COUNTRY PATTERN TWO

Guitar Thigh Rocks— 2 doubles, 4 singles

            —2 doubles, 4 singles

            —2 doubles, 4 singles

    Arms: Pretend you're playing a guitar and
            strum it each time you shift your weight
            and every time you bounce.

Practice 1X

Brief Rest

Break Combo— 1

Practice 1X

LOW WALK

A. Begin with feet together, knees bent, and arms hanging at sides.

B. Walk forward smoothly, R, L, R, L, with knees bent, body straight, and swinging arms in opposition with a snap for each Walk.

JOG BACKWARD AND TURN

A. Begin with feet together and arms in jogging position.

B. Jog 4 Backward (R, L, R, L) with jogging arms.

C. Jog 4 in a FULL CIRCLE RIGHT (R, L, R, L) with jogging arms. This is a *quick* circle.

SLIDES

A. Begin with feet together and arms in jogging position.

B. *MOVING TO THE R:* Hop on L foot and quickly step R foot to the R.

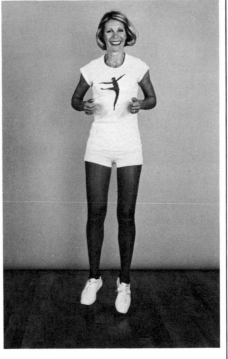

C. Quickly *pick up* L foot to meet R foot with a small jump; weight is now on L foot.

D. CONTINUE: Quickly step R foot to the R and quickly jump L foot to meet R foot. REPEAT TWO MORE TIMES. Reverse directions to do slides *MOVING TO THE L.*

JUMP-FORWARD, JUMP-BACK

A. Begin with feet together and arms in jogging position.

B. Jump-Forward on both feet with knees flexed as you shoot arms up in front of head.

C. Jump-Back on both feet with knees flexed as you pull arms into starting position.

D. CONTINUE: Jump-Forward, Jump-Back.

BENEFITS

- Thighs

- Legs

- Arms

- Waistline

- Aerobic (Jogging, Sliding, and Jumping)

FORM

- Remember to keep back straight on the Low Walk.

- After jogging backward 4, keep in mind that it's 4 jogs in a QUICK CIRCLE R.

- Pick up your feet on the slides.

- Jump-Forward and Jump-Back lightly.

COUNTRY PATTERN THREE

Low Walk—4 forward

    Arms: Swing arms in opposition with a snap for
        each Walk.

Jog—4 backward

    —4 in a FULL QUICK CIRCLE R

    Arms: Jogging position.

Practice 2X's

Brief Rest

Practice 2X's

COUNTRY PATTERN FOUR

Slides—4 *moving to the R* (4 counts)

    Arms: Jogging position.

Jump-Forward, Jump-Back—2 (4 counts)

    Arms: Shoot-up and pull-in for each one.

Slides—4 *moving to the L* (4 counts)

    Arms: Jogging position.

Jump-Forward, Jump-Back—2 (4 counts)

    Arms: Shoot-up and pull-in for each one.

Practice 2X's

Brief Rest

Practice 2X's

GET IT ALL TOGETHER—DANCE!

SUGGESTED MUSIC

"Stargazer" by *Neil Diamond*
"Let Me Be There" by *Olivia Newton-John*
"Walk Right Back" by *Ann Murray*
"Sunflower" by *Glen Campbell*

PATTERN ONE—2 TIMES

Country Hop—R, L, R, L

    Arms: Swing both arms side to side with a snap.

Country Jog—4 forward

             —4 backward

    Arms: Bend elbows with arms in at waist and
          hands at shoulder level, then lean side
          to side as you jog.

PATTERN TWO

Guitar Thigh Rocks—2 doubles, 4 singles

                 —2 doubles, 4 singles

                 —2 doubles, 4 singles

    Arms: Pretend you're playing a guitar and
          strum it each time you shift your weight
          and every time you bounce.

Break Combo—1

PATTERN THREE—2 TIMES

Low Walk—4 forward
   Arms: Swing arms in opposition with a snap for
      each Walk.

Jog—4 backward
   —4 in a FULL QUICK CIRCLE R
   Arms: Jogging position.

PATTERN FOUR—2 TIMES

Slides—4 *moving to the R* (4 counts)
   Arms: Jogging position.

Jump-Forward, Jump-Back—2 (4 counts)
   Arms: Shoot-up and pull-in for each one.

Slides—4 *moving to the L* (4 counts)
   Arms: Jogging position.

Jump-Forward, Jump-Back—2 (4 counts)
   Arms: Shoot-up and pull-in for each one.

Repeat these patterns to music, in any order you want,
until you've danced approximately 2½ – 3 minutes.
TAKE YOUR WORKING HEART RATE.

"STARGAZER"
(Neil Diamond)

AEROBIC DANCE—COUNTRY

> Wait 16 counts
> Country Jog— 4 forward
>   — 4 backward
>   — 4 forward
>   — 4 backward

Pattern ONE*—*2 times*
    Country Hop— R, L, R, L (both arms swing side to side with a snap)
    Country Jog— 4 forward
                 — 4 backward

Pattern TWO —*1 time*
    Guitar Thigh Rocks— 2 doubles, 4 singles
                      — 2 doubles, 4 singles
                      — 2 doubles, 4 singles
    Break Combo— 1

Pattern THREE —*2 times*
    Low Walk— 4 forward (arms swing and snap in opposition)
    Jog— 4 backward (jogging arms)
        — 4 in a FULL CIRCLE R (jogging arms)

Pattern FOUR —*2 times*
    Slides— 4 *moving to the R* (jogging arms)
    Jump-Forward, Jump-Back— 2 (arms shoot-up and pull-in for each one)
    Slides— 4 *moving to the L* (same arms)
    Jump-Forward, Jump-Back— 2 (same arms)

ONE —*2 times*

TWO —*1 time*

THREE —*2 times*

FOUR —*2 times*

ONE —*2 times*

> Guitar Thigh Rocks— 4 doubles, 3 singles**

Hints to help you stay with the music:
 * Vocal begins with this pattern.
** You should end when the music ends.

"LET ME BE THERE"
(Olivia Newton-John)

AEROBIC DANCE— COUNTRY

> ### Wait 16 counts

Pattern ONE*—2 times
    Country Hop— R, L, R, L (both arms swing side to side with a snap)
    Country Jog— 4 forward
            — 4 backward

Pattern TWO—1 time
    Guitar Thigh Rocks— 2 doubles, 4 singles
                 — 2 doubles, 4 singles
                 — 2 doubles, 4 singles

    Break Combo— 1

Pattern THREE—2 times
    Low Walk— 4 forward (arms swing and snap in opposition)
    Jog— 4 backward (jogging arms)
        — 4 in a FULL CIRCLE R (jogging arms)

Pattern FOUR—2 times
    Slides— 4 *moving to the R* (jogging arms)
    Jump-Forward, Jump-Back— 2 (arms shoot-up and pull-in for each one)
    Slides— 4 *moving to the L* (same arms)
    Jump-Forward, Jump-Back— 2 (same arms)

> ### Guitar Thigh Rocks— 2 doubles, 4 singles
> ### Break Combo— 1

ONE —2 times

TWO —1 time

THREE —2 times

FOUR—2 times

ONE —2 times

THREE —2 times

> ### Guitar Thigh Rocks— 6 doubles, 3 singles

Hint to help you stay with the music:
*Vocal begins with this pattern.

BROADWAY!

SUGGESTED MUSIC

"One"
from *A Chorus Line*

"Manhattan Skyline"
from *Saturday Night Fever*

"On Broadway"
by *George Benson*

"Everybody Dance"
by *Chic*

JOG (CIRCLE ARMS)

Jog 8 forward as you circle arms down, up, and around.

A. Begin with feet together and arms in jogging position.

B. RIGHT: Step R as arms Shoot-Out. Draw L foot to R foot as arms pull-in. CONTINUE: Step R as arms Shoot-Out. Draw L foot to R foot as arms pull-in.

A. Begin with feet together and arms in jogging position.

WALK 'N' CLAP

Do 2 Walks in a HALF CIRCLE to the R, then do 2 Walks in place. Clap hands in front of chest on each Walk.

B. RIGHT: Step R with R foot. Draw L foot in to R foot, swinging hips a bit to the R and snapping fingers.

TWO-STEP "SHOOT-OUT"

C.LEFT: Reverse direction and do to L.

ONE-STEP

C. LEFT: Step L with L foot. Draw R foot in to L foot, swinging hips a bit to the L and snapping fingers.

BENEFITS

- Hips
- Legs
- Arms
- Waistline
- Aerobic (Jogging)

FORM

- Lift your knees slightly when you jog and avoid landing high on balls of feet.

- Really stretch when you circle arms down, up, and around.

- Dance the One-Steps with a "Swing it" feeling.

BROADWAY PATTERN ONE

Jog—8 forward

    Arms: Circle arms down, up, and around.

Walk 'n' Clap—2 in a HALF CIRCLE R to face rear

              —2 in place

    Arms: Clap hands in front of chest on each Walk.

Jog—8 to rear

    Arms: Circle arms down, up, and around.

Walk 'n' Clap—2 in a HALF CIRCLE R to face front

              —2 in place

    Arms: Clap hands in front of chest

        on each Walk.

Practice 2X's

Brief Rest

Practice 2X's

BROADWAY PATTERN TWO

Two-Step "Shoot-Out"—R, L,

    Arms: Shoot-Out in front and pull-in; do twice

        for each one.

One-Step—R, L, R, L

    Arms: Jogging position and snap at end of

        each one.

Practice 4X's

JOG WIPERS

A. Begin with feet together and elbows held in at waist with hands in front of chest, palms facing out.

B. Jog, moving both hands with feet (R, then L) like windshield wipers on a car. Try doing 8 Jog Wipers in a FULL CIRCLE R.

KNEELIFTS HOPPING

A. Begin with feet together and hands on hips.

B. Hop on L foot, raising R knee. Bounce feet together.

C. Hop on R foot, raising L knee. Bounce feet together.

KICKS LOW HOPPING

A. Begin with feet together and hands on hips.

B. Kick R foot forward LOW while hopping on L foot. Bounce feet together.

C. Kick L foot forward LOW while hopping on R foot. Bounce feet together.

GET-IT-ALL-TOGETHER COMBO!

A. Begin with feet together and arms in jogging position.

B. RIGHT: Kick R leg out to R side as you hop on L foot and swing arms up at sides to overhead.

C. Bounce 3 times in place with arms in flipped 'V' position.

184

D. Hop on L foot as you lift R knee, and gently slap knee with both hands. Bounce feet together.

E. Hop on L foot again as you lift R knee, and gently slap knee with both hands. Bounce feet together.

F. LEFT: Now, Get-it-all-together on the L by reversing direction and repeating A through E.

BENEFITS

- Hips
- Legs
- Thighs
- Back of Thighs
- Inner Thighs
- Outer Thighs
- Arms
- Waistline
- Aerobic (Jogging, Hopping, and Bouncing)

FORM

- This is "Broadway," so stand tall!
- Don't forget to smile!!
- Happy Dancing!!!

BROADWAY PATTERN THREE

Jog "Wipers"— 8 in a FULL CIRCLE R

Arms: Windshield wiper action R then L for every 2 jogs.

Kneelifts Hopping— 4

Arms: Hands on hips.

Kicks LOW Hopping— 4

Arms: Hands on hips.

Kneelifts Hopping— 4

Arms: Hands on hips.

Practice 2X's

Brief Rest

Practice 2X's

BROADWAY PATTERN FOUR

"Get-It-all-Together" Combo— R, L, R, L

Reminder: Kick Side, swinging arms overhead.

Bounce Three in flipped 'V'.

Kneelift slapping, Bounce Together.

Kneelift slapping (same knee), Bounce Together.

Say: "Kick, Bounce, Bounce, Bounce, Knee, Together, Knee, Together"

Practice 1X

Brief Rest

Practice 1X

GET IT ALL TOGETHER—DANCE!

BROADWAY!

SUGGESTED MUSIC

"One" from *A Chorus Line*
"Manhattan Skyline" from *Saturday Night Fever*
"On Broadway" by *George Benson*
"Everybody Dance" by *Chic*

PATTERN ONE— 2 TIMES

Jog— 8 forward

    Arms: Circle arms down, up, and around.

Walk 'n' Clap— 2 in a HALF CIRCLE R face rear

           — 2 in place

    Arms: Clap hands in front of chest on each Walk.

Jog— 8 to rear

    Arms: Circle arms down, up, and around.

Walk 'n' Clap— 2 in a HALF CIRCLE R to face front

           — 2 in place

    Arms: Clap hands in front of chest on each Walk.

PATTERN TWO— 2 TIMES

Two-Step "Shoot-Out"— R, L

    Arms: Shoot-out in front and pull-in; do twice for each one.

One-Step— R, L, R, L

    Arms: Jogging position and snap at end of each one.

PATTERN THREE

Jog "Wipers"— 8 in a FULL CIRCLE R

Arms: Windshield wiper action

R then L for every 2 jogs.

Kneelifts Hopping— 4

Arms: Hands on hips.

Kicks LOW Hopping— 4

Arms: Hands on hips.

Kneelifts Hopping— 4

Arms: Hands on hips.

PATTERN FOUR

"Get-It-all-Together" Combo— R, L, R, L

Reminder: Kick Side, Swinging arms overhead.

Bounce Three in flipped 'V.'

Kneelift slapping, Bounce Together.

Kneelift slapping (same knee), Bounce Together.

Say: "Kick, Bounce, Bounce, Bounce, Knee, Together, Knee, Together"

Repeat these patterns to music in any order you want until you've danced approximately 3—3½ minutes.
TAKE YOUR WORKING HEART RATE.

"ONE"
(A Chorus Line Original Broadway Cast)

AEROBIC DANCE—BROADWAY

> Wait 8 counts
> Break Combo—1

Pattern ONE—1 time
   Jog—8 forward (circle arms down, up, and around)
   Walk 'n' Clap—2 in a HALF CIRCLE R to face
           —2 in place
   Jog—8 to rear (circle arms down, up, and around)
   Walk 'n' Clap—2 in a HALF CIRCLE R to face front
           —2 in place

Pattern TWO*—2 times
   Two-Step "Shoot-Out"—R, L
   One-Step—R, L, R, L (jogging arms, snap 4 times.)

Pattern THREE—1 time
   Jog "Wipers"—8 in a FULL CIRCLE R
   Kneelifts Hopping—4 (hands on hips)
   Kicks Low Hopping—4 (hands on hips)
   Kneelifts Hopping—4 (hands on hips)

TWO—2 times

THREE—1 time, THEN *Break Combo—1*

Pattern FOUR**—1 time
   "Get-It-All-Together" Combo—R leg, L leg, R leg, L leg
   (Reminder: Say—"Kick, Bounce, Bounce, Bounce, Knee, Together, Knee, Together")

ONE—1 time

FOUR—1 time

ONE—1 time

TWO—2 times (Music speeds up a bit)

THREE—1 time

TWO—2 times

THREE—1 time

TWO—1 time

> Jog "Wipers"—6 in a FULL CIRCLE R
> JUMP FEET TOGETHER WITH A CLAP (there will be extra music,
> but end dance here and take WHR).

Hints to help you stay with the music:
 *Vocal begins with this pattern.
 **When you do this pattern the beginning lyrics are "She walks into a room."

"MANHATTAN SKYLINE"
(Saturday Night Fever Soundtrack)

AEROBIC DANCE—BROADWAY

> Wait 8 counts
> Break Combo—1

Pattern ONE—1 time
   Jog—8 forward (circle arms down, up, and around)
   Walk 'n' Clap—2 in a HALF CIRCLE R to face rear
            —2 in place
   Jog—8 to rear (circle arms down, up, and around)
   Walk 'n' Clap—2 in a HALF CIRCLE R to face front
            —2 in place

Pattern TWO—2 times
   Two-Step "Shoot-Out"—R, L
   One-Step—R, L, R, L (jogging arms, snap 4 times)

Pattern THREE—2 times*
   Jog "Wipers"—8 in a FULL CIRCLE R
   Kneelifts Hopping—4 (hands on hips)
   Kicks Low Hopping—4 (hands on hips)
   Kneelifts Hopping—4 (hands on hips)

ONE—1 time

Pattern FOUR—1 time
   "Get-It-All-Together" Combo—R leg, L leg, R leg, L leg
   (Reminder: Say—"Kick, Bounce, Bounce, Bounce, Knee, Together, Knee, Together")

> Jog "Wipers"—8 in a FULL CIRCLE R
> Break Combo—1

ONE—1 time

TWO—2 times

THREE—2 times

ONE—1 time

FOUR—1 time, THEN *Break Combo—1 (there will be extra music, but end dance here and take WHR).*

Hint to help you stay with the music:
*The instrumental music is the same every time you do Pattern THREE.

THE COOL-DOWN

The Cool-down routine is a slow dance with graceful stretching movements that gradually reduce the intensity of your workout and help your body wind down. After the dance, do your calf stretches until it's time to take your 5-minute recovery heart rate. If this rate is greater than 120 per minute, dance at a lower level during your next workout. Don't sit down until your heart rate is 120 or less.

SUGGESTED MUSIC

"Hopelessly Devoted to You"
by *Olivia Newton-John*

"Looks Like We Made It"
by *Barry Manilow*

"Lady-Oh"
by *Neil Diamond*

"When You're Loved"
by *Debbie Boone*

WALK

Walk landing on the ball of your foot first. Swing arms naturally in opposition. Also, try walking 8 steps as you circle arms up and around one time.

LUNGE SIDE

A. Begin with feet together, knees relaxed, and hands clasped in back.

B. Lunge to the R with R leg, bending both knees. Return to starting position. Hands are clasped in back.

C. Lunge to the L with L leg, bending both knees. Return to starting position. Hands are clasped in back.

TWO STEP "CIRCLE UP"

A. Begin with feet together and arms hanging at sides.

B. RIGHT: Step to R with R foot and draw L foot to R foot. Arms cross and begin to "Circle Up."

C. Step to R with R foot and draw L foot to R foot. Arms finish circling up and around.

D. LEFT: Reverse directions and do to L.

LUNGE FORWARD

A. Begin with feet together and hands clasped in back.

B. Lunge Forward on R foot, bending both knees. Return to starting position. Hands are clasped in back. Repeat with L foot.

PATTERN ONE

Walk— 4 toward R shoulder

    Arms: Swing naturally in opposition.

Lunge Side— R, L

    Arms: Hands clasped in back.

Practice 4X's to make a square

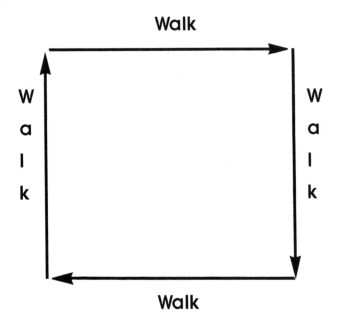

PATTERN TWO

Two-Step— R, L
   Arms: Circle arms up and around once on
         each Two-Step.

Lunge Forward— R, L, R, L
   Arms: Hands clasped behind.

Practice 2X's

STEP-OUT, CROSS-OVER

A. Begin with feet together and arms hanging at sides.

B. MOVING TO R: Step to the R with R foot as arms shoot-up to 'V' position.

C. Lightly draw the L foot to cross-over the R foot as arms pull-in to chest. CONTINUE: Step-out to R; Draw L foot to cross-over R foot; Step-out to R; Draw L foot to cross-over R foot.

D. MOVING TO L: Step to the L with L foot as arms shoot-up to 'V' position. Lightly draw the R foot to cross-over the L foot as arms pull-in to body. CONTINUE: Step-out to L; Draw R foot to cross-over L foot; Step-out to L; Draw R foot to cross-over L foot.

LUNGE SIDE "PRESENT"

A. Begin with feet together and arms in jogging position.

B. RIGHT: Lunge to the R with R leg, bending both knees. Arms present forward.

C. Return to starting position, as arms pull-in to chest.

D. LEFT: Lunge to the L with L leg, bending both knees as arms present forward. Return to starting position, as arms pull-in to chest.

PATTERN THREE

Step-Out, Cross-Over— 3 moving to R
Arms: Shoot-up to 'V' position, then pull-in for
each one.

Lunge Side "Present"— R
Arms: Present forward, then pull-in to chest.

Step-Out, Cross-Over— 3 moving to L
Arms: Shoot-up to 'V' position, then pull-in for
each one.

Lunge Side "Present"— L

Arms: Present forward, then pull-in to chest.

Practice 4X's

PATTERN FOUR

Walk— 8 in a FULL CIRCLE R
    Arms: Both arms circle up and
           around once, SLOW.

Lunge Forward— R, L, R, L
    Arms: Hands clasped in back.

Practice 2X's

GET IT ALL TOGETHER—DANCE!

THE COOL-DOWN

SUGGESTED MUSIC

"Hopelessly Devoted to You" by *Olivia Newton-John*

"Looks Like We Made It" by *Barry Manilow*

"Lady-Oh" by *Neil Diamond*

"When You're Loved" by *Debbie Boone*

PATTERN ONE—4 TIMES

Walk—4 toward R shoulder

    Arms: Swing naturally in opposition.

Lunge Side—R, L

    Arms: Hands clasped in back.

PATTERN TWO—2 TIMES

Two-Step—R, L

    Arms: Circle arms up and around once
          on each Two-Step.

Lunge Forward—R, L, R, L

    Arms: Hands clasped behind.

PATTERN THREE—2 TIMES

Step-Out, Cross-Over— 3 moving to R
   Arms: Shoot-up to 'V' position, then pull-in for
      each one.

Lunge Side "Present"— R
   Arms: Present forward, then pull-in to chest.

Step-Out, Cross-Over— 3 moving to L
   Arms: Shoot-up to 'V' position, then pull-in for
      each one.

Lunge Side "Present"— L
   Arms: Present forward, then pull-in to chest.

PATTERN FOUR—1 TIME

Walk— 8 in a FULL CIRCLE R
   Arms: Both arms circle up and around
      once, SLOW.

Lunge Forward— R, L, R, L
   Arms: Hands clasped in back.

* Ending: Kneebend Sweep— 2 (4 counts each)

> *Before doing the ending repeat Patterns One
> and Three as before to complete "The Cool-down."
> **TAKE YOUR RECOVERY HEART RATE**

"HOPELESSLY DEVOTED TO YOU"
(Olivia Newton-John)

COOL-DOWN DANCE

> Wait 8 slow counts
> Lunge Forward—R, L, R, L (hands clasped in back)

Pattern ONE*—4 times (to make a square)
  Walk—4 toward R shoulder (arms swing low in opposition)
  Lunge Side—R, L (hands clasped in back)

Pattern TWO—2 times
  Two-Step "Circle Up"—R, L
  Lunge Forward—R, L, R, L (hands clasped in back)

> Walk—8 in a FULL CIRCLE R (circle arms up and around, once, slow)

Pattern THREE**—2 times
  Step-Out, Cross-Over—3 moving to R (shoot-up to 'V,' then pull-in for each one)
  Lunge Side "Present"—R
  Step-Out, Cross-Over—3 moving to L (same arms)
  Lunge Side "Present"—L

Pattern FOUR—1 time
  Walk—8 in a FULL CIRCLE R (circle arms up and around, once, slow)
  Lunge Forward—R, L (hands clasped in back)

ONE—4 times (to make a square)

> Walk—8 in a FULL CIRCLE R (circle arms up and around, once, slow)

THREE—2 times

> Walk—8 in a FULL CIRCLE R (circle arms up and around, once, slow)
> Kneebend Sweep—2 (4 counts each)

Hints to help you stay with the music:
  * Vocal begins with this pattern.
  ** The beginning lyrics are "There's nowhere to hide." Step-Out on word "no."

204

"LOOKS LIKE WE MADE IT"
(Barry Manilow)

COOL-DOWN DANCE

> Wait 8 slow counts
> Lunge Forward — R, L, R, L (hands clasped in back)

Pattern ONE* — 1 time (to make a square)
  Walk — 4 toward R shoulder (arms swing low in opposition)
  Lunge Side — R, L, R, L (hands clasped in back)
  Walk — 4 toward R shoulder
  Lunge Side — R, L, R, L
  Walk — 4 toward R shoulder
  Lunge Side — R, L
  Walk — 4 toward R shoulder
  Lunge Side — R, L

Pattern THREE** — 2 times
  Step-Out, Cross-Over — 3 moving to R (shoot-up to 'V,' then pull in for each one)
  Lunge Side "Present" — R
  Step-Out, Cross-Over — 3 moving to L (same arms)
  Lunge Side "Present" — L

> Lunge Forward — R, L, R, L (hands clasped in back)

ONE — 1 time (to make a square)

THREE — 2 times

Pattern TWO — 1 time
  Two-Step "Circle Up" — R, L, R, L
  Lunge Forward — R, L (shoot-up to 'V,' then pull-in for each one)

THREE — 2 times

> Two-Step "Circle Up" — R, L, R, L
> Kneebend Sweep — 1 (7 counts; music fades)

Hints to help you stay with the music:
  * Vocal begins with this pattern.
  ** The beginning lyrics are "Looks like we made it." Step-Out on word "made."

205

3

DANCING FOR YOUR LIFETIME FITNESS

PLANNING FOR LIFETIME FITNESS

Now that you've followed my program for 12 weeks, you've met the challenge and experienced the fun of learning Aerobic Dancing. You know how it feels to be physically fit, and the key now is to MAINTAIN that fitness with a combination of regular Aerobic Dancing workouts, rhythmic sit-ups, other aerobic-based activities, and sensible eating habits. Remember: *you can store fat, but you can't store physical fitness: it must be renewed regularly*. A committee of the American College of Sports Medicine notes that a 4-to-12 week layoff from a regular exercise program will cause a 50 percent loss of condition, and beyond 12 weeks one is essentially starting all over again.

AEROBIC DANCING AS A YEAR-ROUND FITNESS PROGRAM

Once you've completed the first 12-week learning progression, there are numerous ways you can continue to use this book to organize Aerobic Dancing into a basic year-round conditioner done at home. Here are three suggested approaches:

A Second 12-Week Program: Remember, every Aerobic Dance (plus the Warm-up and Cool-down) has been choreographed to two different songs. So if you've memorized the first choreographed dance for each style, you can learn the second ones over the next 12 weeks. The steps are the same, but you dance them in slightly different patterns to new music, so you'll feel like you're doing completely different dances.

Try to learn one new dance a week, at the beginning of your Aerobic Dancing segment, and then complete this segment by dancing dances you already know. By taking this approach, you maximize the aerobic stage of every workout and are easily able to keep your working heart rate in your WHR range. Moreover, now that you are in better shape, you will be able to dance at a higher level through most of the workout. Another nice thing is that you never have to shelve your favorite dances as you gain more proficiency and greater fitness.

Third 12-Week Program: Taking all the choreographed dances that you know—which may be as many as 20—you'll have more than enough variety in music and dance styles to organize workouts that will keep you emotionally involved and physically challenged. Just select six to eight dances per workout and strive for about 20 to 30 minutes of *continuous dancing*, taking your WHR after each dance. Try to get the most out of each dance and each workout. For example, dance particular steps with a bit more style, smoothness, and expression. And instead of "walking" between dances, "jog." Also, make sure you go through the proper Flexibility, Warm-up, and Cool-down routines.

Fourth 12-Week Program: See how much fun it is to create your own dances and blend them together in personalized workouts. Drawing on the dozens of different steps and patterns you know, match them to music you've selected from the Music Index (page 222) and "dance your own dances" for about 30 minutes. Just remember to dance vigorously and take your WHR every 3–3½ minutes. You can keep your program updated and continually challenging by creating a new dance whenever a song comes out that you like.

Join an Aerobic Dancing Class: Check the phone book for an Aerobic Dancing program in your local area. New 12-week sessions start throughout the year, with *new music and new dances*. Since every session is performed at an individual's own level of skill and fitness, new students can enter any class and be successful. At the same time, motivation and challenge are sustained for continuing students. In fact, our re-enrollment rate is about 80 percent, as students find that Aerobic Dancing is their way of staying in shape year-round.

TONING THE ABDOMINAL MUSCLES

Since most vigorous activities, including Aerobic Dancing, fail to give the abdominal muscles a sufficient workout in terms of acquiring a firm stomach, supplemental situp exercises are recommended.

The rhythmic, bent-knee situps described here should be done five days a week for maximum results. Begin with as many situps as you can do *comfortably* and *without strain*, and then gradually increase the amount with an eventual goal of 30 situps each time. I feel that rhythmic bent-knee situps are preferable to the traditional straight-leg situps because (1) they are safer—straight-leg situps may cause lower back stress and painful knee strain—and (2) they give the abdominal muscles a much better workout.

Let's face it: it's hard to really *enjoy* doing situps. But they can be more enjoyable when you

RHYTHMIC SITUP

A. Begin by lying on your back with legs bent and with feet flat on floor or resting on heels. Extend arms above head with elbows relaxed.

B. Curl up slowly, tucking head first, and touch knees lightly with fingertips. This is count one.

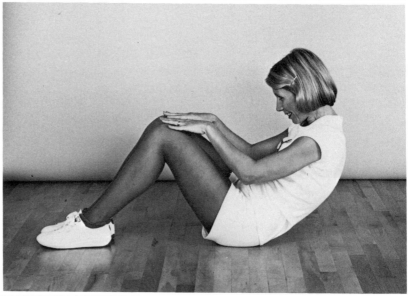

use music or television as a background. Just remember that if you want to have a flatter, firmer stomach, then situps are only one of three maintenance requirements. The other two are:

1. *Muscle Control.* As you develop stronger abdominal muscles through situps, you must learn to *use* this strength. Otherwise, these muscles will begin to sag. Continually think about contracting your stomach, pulling "in and up" as you "stand tall."

2. *Calorie Control.* If you're storing excess fat in the abdominal area, the muscle strength and muscle control you acquire will not give you a flat stomach. You simply cannot squeeze three pounds into a two-pound can! That excess fat must be burned off by expending more calories through exercise than you are taking in through eating.

C. Bend forward and touch toes lightly with fingertips. Count two.

D. Touch knees again (count three). Return to starting position on count four.

Note: This is a SLOW, CONTROLLED 4-COUNT rhythmic situp that you do at your own pace. The abdominal muscles get more exercise if you lower your body at a moderate rate rather than quickly.

Suggested Music: Shadow Dancing (Andy Gibb), Blue Bayou (Linda Ronstadt), Can't Smile Without You (Barry Manilow), Both Sides Now (Neil Diamond).

If you want to do additional flexibility movements, try the following exercises. Remember, there shouldn't be any ballistic (bouncing) or forced action to these movements. They can be combined with rhythmic situps and done before an Aerobic Dancing workout or other activity.

STATIC STRETCH FORWARD
Stretches inner thigh muscles, hamstrings, and back

A. Sit in a medium 'V' stride with legs straight but not locked, and toes upright with arms extended forward.

B. Move upper body slowly forward, bending at the waist, and hold approximately 16 slow counts with arms stretched out in front, palms facing forward and your chin up. Be sure to keep back and legs straight. Return to starting position. Do a minimum of 2 stretches.

STATIC STRETCH SIDE
Stretches inner thigh muscles, hamstrings (backs of thighs), and each side of back

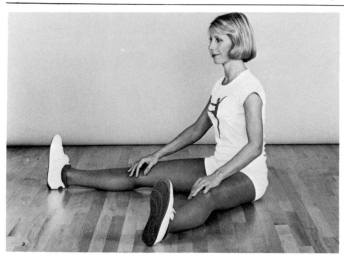

A. Begin seated in a medium 'V' stride with legs straight, but not locked, and toes upright.

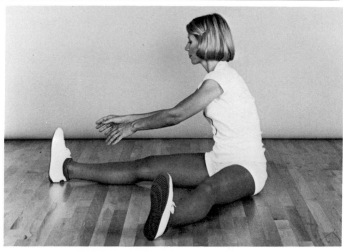

B. Turn upper body to face right foot and bend gently toward this foot.

C. Grasp some place on the lower leg that gives you a *gentle* stretch and hold for approximately 16 slow counts. It's not necessary to touch your forehead to your knee or leg.

D. Sit up and reach gently to left foot and stretch. Do a minimum of 2 stretches for each leg.

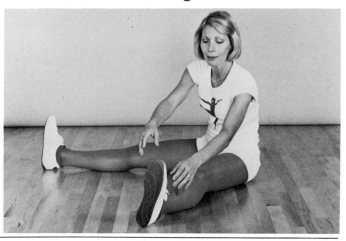

WRINGER

Stretches neck, lower back, hamstring of lifted leg, and increases hip flexibility

A. Begin by lying on your back, arms out at sides shoulder height, and knees slightly flexed with weight on heels.

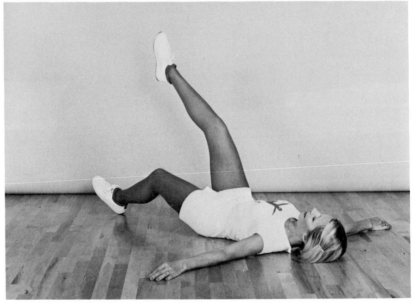

B. Raise right leg, keeping knee slightly flexed, and stretch it across body to touch foot to floor. Slightly turn head opposite of foot action.

Raise right leg back over your body and return to starting position. Reverse directions for left leg. Do 8 wringers alternating legs.

LYING SIDE LEG RAISER
Stretches inner and outer thigh and ankle

A. Lie on side with head resting comfortably on arm. Place other hand on floor in front of you for support.

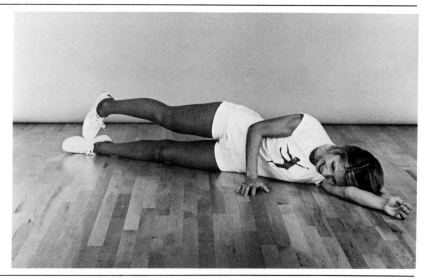

B. Lift top leg between 24–36 inches with toe always pointed toward foot on floor. Lower your leg so toe gently touches arch of foot on floor. Do 8 leg raises with each leg.

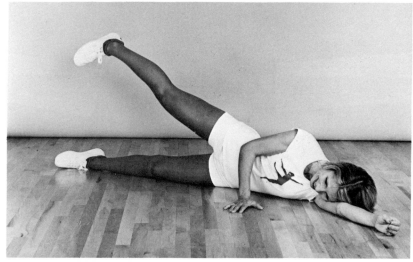

ANKLE STRETCHER
Stretches ankle and opposite calf muscles and hamstring.

Stand four feet from wall, feet together and hands on wall at shoulder height. Alternately flex one knee by rising up on toes of foot, then repeat with other foot.

WALL STRETCH
Stretches the achilles tendon

Standing 3 to 4 feet from a wall, pigeon-toed, place hands on wall at shoulder height and lean forward until forehead touches wall. Feet remain flat on floor. Back is kept straight and buttocks tucked in. By strengthening the tendons, you ease strain on the shins and help prevent shin splints.

CALF AND ANKLE STRETCHER
Stretches the calf and ankle muscles

Place hands shoulder high against wall and bend elbows until forehead rests against wall. Stretch one leg at a time or both. If both, keep legs straight, feet flat on floor. Our instructors have found that this stretching exercise, like the ankle stretcher and the wall stretch, is beneficial in preventing shin splints.

THE 3-WORKOUTS-A-WEEK CONCEPT

Medical research is showing that if you want to insure proper cardiovascular fitness, you should plan a minimum of three aerobic workouts every week. If you're following my program twice a week, you can either organize your own dancing workout this third day, or select another activity that also uses large muscle groups, can be maintained continuously, and is rhythmical and aerobic in nature. Whatever you choose to do, the main point is that these third-day activities help keep you motivated to stay active week after week, whatever the time of year.

Although this third day of aerobic activity is everyone's *goal*, just by dancing two times a week you're going to realize fitness benefits and figure improvement and you're going to feel better. But you may find that you don't improve beyond these initial fitness benefits, because there's too much time between workouts. Happily, you probably won't settle for remaining sedentary the rest of the week once you discover Aerobic Dancing. Most of my students find that it gives them so much energy and makes them feel so good about themselves that it's the beginning of a whole new world. They want to become physically active in other ways, and they're encouraged to try new sports and exercise activities.

In your own case, as you increase fitness and muscle tone you will be more likely to play racquetball or buy a jump rope or set aside an afternoon for jogging or brisk walking. You will *want* to be more active, and your third day will come naturally. In fact, you may already have this workout built into your life. Before, it was insufficient as a physical conditioner, but now—coupled with Aerobic Dancing—you have a complete fitness program!

OTHER SUGGESTED AEROBIC ACTIVITIES

Although you may want to make Aerobic Dancing your third workout each week, to me it's only *one* of many activities that are fun and will keep you aerobically fit. I've also found that *variety* is the best way to prevent boredom and help you stay committed to an overall lifetime fitness program. Following are three aerobic activities that you might want to consider because you can do them by yourself practically anywhere. They don't require special equipment or facilities, and they won't cost you a lot of money.

Jogging: An indoor fitness program like Aerobic Dancing is exhilarating, convenient, and effective. But when the weather permits, it's fun to get outdoors and jog. Even with all the dancing I do, I look forward to running at least 45 minutes 5 days a week, whether I'm at home or traveling.

There are literally dozens of books on the market that can tell you all you might want to know about jogging, but here are some general guidelines which can get you started:

1. Wear comfortable, loose clothing and properly fitting shoes with good arch support, heel cushioning, and resilient soles.

2. Choose grass, asphalt, or a track to jog on; avoid concrete—it's the worst surface.

3. Before you start, do the Flexibility routine you've learned in Aerobic Dancing and walk a bit.

4. Breathe normally and easily. If you can't talk as you jog, you're overdoing it.

5. Keep your arms relaxed, with your body erect and in good alignment. Don't lean forward.

6. Just as in dancing, avoid running high on the balls of your feet.

7. Cool down by walking for at least 5 minutes, and then do your Calf stretches.

Brisk Walking: Walking can be fun for almost everyone. Just make sure you stride along at a brisk pace. As President of Aerobic Dancing, Inc., I find it hard to sit around in meetings, so I've started walking meetings of one to two hours. This works great with up to three people, and we're never interrupted by the telephone. At the same time, we're getting exercise, burning off calories, and everyone is more alert.

Rope Skipping: An Aerobic Dancing student who had recently shed 20 pounds was talking excitedly about her upcoming vacation when a second student asked her if she wasn't worried about gaining weight while traveling and having to miss Aerobic Dancing classes. "Of course not," she said smugly. "I've packed my rope." She knew that rope skipping would help balance her possible increased caloric intake and maintain her newly-gained energy reserves so she could vacation to the hilt!

Rope skipping is one of the most effective and convenient aerobic exercises you can choose to supplement your Aerobic Dancing workouts. It's something you can do at any time and in any relatively small area, whether you're housebound or in a hotel room. Rope skipping improves your coordination, conditions your cardiovascular system, and is especially beneficial for the muscles of the chest, upper arms, hips, thighs, and calves since it involves overall muscle action.

Following are some guidelines for beginning a rope skipping program:

1. Wear comfortable clothing and shoes with cushioned heels and good support. AVOID skipping on any type of concrete surface.

2. Adjust rope for your height. When you stand with the rope under your heels, it should be long enough to reach slightly above your waistline. This allows you to skip with ease and proper body alignment.

3. Begin by doing the Flexibility routine you've learned.

4. Don't lean forward or backward as you skip, and make sure your abdominals are held in and up, and your chin stays level.

5. Try to turn the rope with your elbows held close to your body, using mainly lower arm and wrist movement.

6. It will take some time to become proficient, so be patient and go slowly. Even if you are fit, you will be trying to master a new skill while using your muscles in a new way.

7. At first, try to skip for one minute without stopping. Walk around to catch your breath and then try for another minute of skipping. When you can skip continuously for about three minutes, pick out some favorite songs for accompaniment—just as you might do in Aerobic Dancing. Monitor your heart rate after each song and work up to a 15-minute session.

8. Cool down by walking slowly and doing your Calf Stretches.

ROPE- SKIPPING

Try these different methods of rope skipping:

BASIC SKIP: Skip, alternating feet and swinging your free leg back. (a) Skip over the rope with R foot as L foot swings back. (b) Hop on R foot as L foot swings forward. (c) Skip over the rope with L foot as R foot swings back. (d) Hop on L foot as R foot swings forward.

BASIC BOUNCE: Jump over the rope with both feet together. Keep your knees relaxed and land on the balls of your feet—not on your toes. Add a small bounce between jumps for a more rhythmic movement.

ROCKING SKIP: Place R foot forward. Without using the rope, rock forward on R foot, then rock back on L foot. After a little rocking practice, try rocking over the rope on every forward rock. Change to L foot forward by doing a few Basic Bounces in between R rocks and L rocks.

WAISTLINE SKIP: Use the following rope motion as you do the Basic Skip: Holding ends of rope, place arms forward with wrists together. Beginning down and to the R, make a figure eight so the rope hits the ground to your R side, then to your L side. The larger your figure eight, the more you are exercising your waistline. This is also a good variation to use for a change of pace when you are tired of skipping OVER the rope.

ADD MOVEMENT: Travel forward or backward doing the Basic Skip or the Rocking Skip. Travel side to side, with your body forward, doing the Basic Bounce.

DIET AND EXERCISE

Whether or not you have a weight problem, the winning combination for maintaining or reaching a healthy weight is simple: *less food and more activity.* "The difference between overweight people and normal weight people is not only how much they eat, but how much they move," says Dr. Frank Katch, head of the Exercise Science Department of the University of Massachusetts.

I also feel that dieting alone is not the most effective method of losing weight, nor the healthiest. If you lose weight by dieting, gain it back, then lose it again, and so on, you're on a "roller coaster cycle" that not only is depressing but is bad for your skin and muscle tone. Instead of constantly dieting and re-dieting, it's better to learn to balance food intake *and* energy output. As one of our students observed, "I knew I couldn't lose weight just by watching what I ate. I needed a regular exercise program, and Aerobic Dancing was it."

Hints to Cut and Burn Calories:

1. Increase your activity level and cut down on calories. It's a lot faster to take off pounds when you are eating *less and* exercising more.

2. Add more activity as you go about your day. Choose stairs over elevators. Walk short distances rather than riding. Move with a peppy step!

3. Get high-calorie, nutritionally empty snacks out of the house, or at least out of sight. Take note: ½ cup of peanuts equals 420 calories.

4. Keep low-calorie snacks prepared and readily available.

5. Plan your day so you're in the kitchen a minimal amount of time. If necessary, have the telephone moved out of the kitchen so food won't be so handy while you're on the phone.

6. Plan a day when you're going to have a favorite treat. Wait until then to indulge.

7. Divert your attention from food by reading a good book instead of nibbling.

8. Put smaller portions on your plate and eat slowly.

9. Eating smaller, more frequent meals is an effective weight control method for some people.

10. Get rid of leftovers. It's better to waste a bit of food than to see it on your body as excess weight.

11. Include more fish and poultry in your menus. Remember that boiled, baked, and broiled foods are lower in calories than fried or sauteed foods.

12. Trim fat from meat and remove skin from poultry.

13. Try to increase daily consumption of salads and vegetables and decrease consumption of meat.

14. Resist cocktails. Alcohol tends to stimulate your appetite and lower your will power to resist food.

15. Educate yourself about how many calories you use each day, then adjust your eating habits to stay within this calorie limit. This will allow you to take the approach of one of our students, who said, "When I come to the class I know I can have dessert with dinner and not gain weight. If I miss class—no dessert!"

STRESS AND EXERCISE

When your body is under emotional or physical stress, it releases the hormone adrenaline, commonly referred to as the "fight or flight" hormone. If you're not on a regular exercise program, adrenaline tends to accumulate in your body. This excess adrenaline can contribute to a sense of fatigue and affect your emotional response and mood. If you feel dragged down after a hard day's work, it may be that your system has been flooded with adrenaline. Exercise increases your metabolism, which uses up this excess adrenaline. This helps explain why exercise is so *energizing.* Instead of having a listless, helpless feeling, your fitness workouts will make you feel in charge and on top of things. What's good for your muscles is also good for your mind!

THE CHALLENGE OF PHYSICAL FITNESS

Physical fitness is like sex appeal—if you have it you know it. It's being high on life most of the time. It's having unbridled energy and feeling alive all day and into the evening. It's being happier with family and friends because you're happier about yourself. If you're fit, you'll look better and feel better, and that creates a glow of vitality. And once you've been fit, you're *addicted* for life.

The challenge, however, is to motivate yourself to get fit and to stay fit. When experiences in movement become personally expressive, personally satisfying, and a joyful release, then you become "addicted" to movement, and you will not live without it.

SO HAVE FUN, AND KEEP FIT!

MUSIC INDEX

TITLE	ARTIST	ALBUM TITLE	RECORD CO.	ALBUM NO.
FLEXIBILITY:				
"I Write The Songs"	Barry Manilow	"Barry Manilow—Greatest Hits"	Arista Records	A2L 8601
"If You Know What I Mean"	Neil Diamond	"Beautiful Noise"	Columbia Records	PC 33965
"Just The Way You Are"	Billy Joel	"The Stranger"	Columbia Records	JC 34987
"(Our Love) Don't Throw It All Away"	Andy Gibb	"Andy Gibb / Shadow Dancing"	RSO Records	RS-1-3034
WARM-UP:				
"Higher And Higher"	Rita Collidge	"Anytime . . . Anywhere"	A & M Records	A&M SP4616
"How Deep Is Your Love"	Bee Gees	"Saturday Night Fever"	RSO Records	RS-2-4001
"There Will Be Love"	Lou Rawls	"When You Hear Lou, You've Heard It All"	Philadelphia International Records	JZ 35036
"Mandy"	Barry Manilow	"Barry Manilow—Greatest Hits"	Arista Records	A2L 8601
CHARLESTON:				
"Sweet, Sweet Smile"	Carpenters	"Passage"	A & M Records	A&M SP4703
"Da Doo Ron Ron"	Shaun Cassidy	"Shaun Cassidy"	Warner Bros. Records	BS 3067
"Southern Nights"	Glen Campbell	"Southern Nights"	Capitol Records	SO-11601
HUSTLE:				
"You Should Be Dancing"	Bee Gees	"Saturday Night Fever"	RSO Records	RS-2-4001
"Y.M.C.A."	Village People	"Cruisin' "	Casablanca Records	NBLP 7118
"It's A Miracle"	Barry Manilow	"Barry Manilow—Greatest Hits"	Arista Records	A2L 8601
"You Make Lovin' Fun"	Fleetwood Mac	"Rumors"	Warner Bros. Records	BSK 3010
BOOGIE:				
"Jump Shout Boogie"	Barry Manilow	"Barry Manilow—Greatest Hits"	Arista Records	A2L 8601
"Johnny B. Goode"	John Denver	"John Denver"	RCA Records	AQLI-3075
"Rock & Roll Party Queen"	Louis St. Louis	"Grease"	RSO Records	RS-2-4002
"In The Mood"	Ray Coniff	"The Happy Sounds of Ray Coniff"	Columbia Records	KC 33139
ROCK:				
"Desirée"	Neil Diamond	"I'm Glad You're Here With Me Tonight"	Columbia Records	JC 34990
"Don't Stop"	Fleetwood Mac	"Rumors"	Warner Bros. Records	BSK 3010
"Love Will Keep Us Together"	Capt. & Tennille	"Love Will Keep Us Together"	A & M Records	A&M SP4552
"That's When The Music Takes Me"	Neil Sedaka	"Solitaire"	RCA Records	APL1-1790
STRETCH:				
"Come Share My Love"	Debbie Boone	"Midstream	Warner Bros. Records	BSK 3130
"Beautiful Music"	Barry Manilow	"Barry Manilow—Greatest Hits"	Arista Records	A2L 8601
"An Everlasting Love"	Andy Gibb	"Andy Gibb / Shadow Dancing"	RSO Records	RS-1-3034
"Wayward Wind"	Crystal Gayle	"When I Dream"	United Artists	UA-LA858-H
DISCO:				
"Le Freak"	Chic	"C'est Chic"	Atlantic Records	SD 19209
"Disco Inferno"	The Trammps	"Saturday Night Fever"	RSO Records	RS-2-4001
"Last Dance"	Donna Summer	"Live And More"	Casablanca Records	NBLP 7119-2
"New York City Rhythm"	Barry Manilow	"Barry Manilow—Greatest Hits"	Arista Records	A2L 8601

COUNTRY:

"Stargazer"	Neil Diamond	"Beautiful Noise"	Columbia Records	PC 33965
"Let Me Be There"	Olivia Newton-John	"Olivia Newton-John's Greatest Hits	MCA Records	MCA-3028
"Walk Right Back"	Ann Murray	"Keep It That Way"	Capitol Records	ST-11743
"Sunflower"	Glen Campbell	"Southern Nights"	Capitol Records	SO-11601

BROADWAY:

"One" (Finale)	Orig. Broadway Cast	"A Chorus Line"	Columbia Records	PS 33581
"Manhattan Skyline"	The Trammps	"Saturday Night Fever"	RSO Records	RS-2-4001
"On Broadway"	George Benson	"Weekend In L.A."	Warner Bros. Records	2B-3139
"Everybody Dance"	Chic	"Chic"	Atlantic Records	SD 19153

COOL-DOWN:

"Hopelessly Devoted To You"	Olivia Newton-John	"Olivia Newton-John's Greatest Hits"	MCA Records	MCA-3028
"Looks Like We Made It"	Barry Manilow	"Barry Manilow—Greatest Hits"	Arista Records	A2L 8601
"Lady Oh"	Neil Diamond	"Beautiful Noise"	Columbia Records	PC 33965
"When You're Loved"	Debbie Boone	"Midstream"	Warner Bros. Records	BSK 3130

SITUPS:

"Shadow Dancing"	Andy Gibb	"Andy Gibb/Shadow Dancing"	RSO Records	RS-1-3034
"Blue Bayou"	Linda Ronstadt	"Simple Dreams"	Elektra-Asylum Records	Asylum 6E-104
"Can't Smile Without You"	Barry Manilow	"Barry Manilow—Greatest Hits"	Arista Records	A2L 8601
"Both Sides Now"	Neil Diamond	"Touching You, Touching Me"	Universal City Records	93071

STEP INDEX